Be a Better Time Manager

Published by :
Lotus Press Publishers & Distributors

Be a Better Time Manager

B.K. Pathak

Lotus Press

4735/22, Prakash Deep Building
Ansari Road, Darya Ganj,
New Delhi - 110002

Lotus Press : Publishers & Distributors
Unit No. 220, 2nd Floor, 4735/22, Prakash Deep Building,
Ansari Road, Darya Ganj, New Delhi- 110002
Ph.: 41325510, 23280047, 98118-38000
• E-mail : lotuspress1984@gmail.com
www.lotuspress.co.in

Be a Better Time Manager

ISBN: 978-81-8382-280-0

Printed & Published by : **Lotus Press Publishers & Distributors,** New Delhi-02

PREFACE

Managing time well enables an individual to do the right thing at the right time. Time management plays a pivotal role in one's personal as well as professional life. Every organization works on deadlines. An individual constantly needs to be on his toes to finish off assignments within stipulated time frame. It is essential for employees to understand the value of time for them to do well and make a mark of their own at the workplace.

Be a Better Time Manager is written for everyone who would like to manage their time better and is full of practical tips and techniques. It will provide insights into how and why time needs to be managed and shows the reader how to keep from being snowed under by information overload, tight deadlines and constant interruptions.

This book avoids the mechanistic approach and looks at the psychological and behavioural aspects of time management as well as the more practical ways of managing time more efficiently and effectively. Unless attitudes, beliefs and habits are examined, argues this book, no 'system' will work. This book, therefore, tackles the roots of time management problems and offers sensible, tailor-made solutions. It is a fast track guide to becoming a competent and better time manager.

B. K. Pathak

CONTENTS

1

IMPORTANCE OF TIME MANAGEMENT

Time management refers to managing time effectively so that the right time is allocated to the right activity. Effective time management allows individuals to assign specific time slots to activities as per their importance. Ask yourself which activity is more important and how much time should be allocated to the same? Know which work should be done earlier and which can be done a little later.

Time management plays a very important role not only in organizations but also in our personal lives.

COMPONENTS OF TIME MANAGEMENT

Time Management includes:

- Effective Planning
- Setting Goals and Objectives
- Setting Deadlines
- Delegation of Responsibilities
- Prioritizing Activities as per their Importance
- Spending the Right Time on the Right Activity

Effective Planning

Plan your day well in advance. Prepare a To Do List or a "TASK PLAN". Jot down the important activities that need to be done in a single day against the time that should be allocated to each activity. High Priority work should come on top followed by those which do not need much of your importance at the moment. Complete pending tasks one by one. Do not begin fresh work unless you have finished your previous task. Tick the ones you have already completed. Ensure you finish the tasks within the stipulated time frame.

Setting Goals and Objectives

Working without goals and targets in an organization would be similar to a situation where the captain of the ship loses his way in the sea. Yes, you would be lost. Set targets for yourself and make sure they are realistic ones and achievable.

Setting Deadlines

Set deadlines for yourself and strive hard to complete tasks ahead of the deadlines. Do not wait for your superiors to ask you everytime.Learn to take ownership of work. One person who can best set the deadlines is you yourself. Ask yourself how much time needs to be devoted to a particular task and for how many days. Use a planner to mark the important dates against the set deadlines.

Delegation of Responsibilities

Learn to say "NO" at workplace. Don't do everything on your own. There are other people as well. One should not accept something which he knows is difficult for him. The roles and responsibilities must be delegated as per interest and specialization of employees for them to finish tasks within deadlines. A person who does not have knowledge about something needs more time than someone who knows the work well.

Prioritizing Tasks

Prioritise the tasks as per their importance and urgency. Know the difference between important and urgent work. Identify which tasks should be done within a day, which all should be done within a month and so on. Tasks which are most important should be done earlier.

Spending the Right Time on Right Activity

Develop the habit of doing the right thing at the right time. Work done at the wrong time is not of much use. Don't waste a complete day on something which can be done in an hour or so. Also keep some time separate for your personal calls or checking updates on Facebook or Twitter. After all human being is not a machine.

For Effective Time Management one needs to be:

- *Organized*—Avoid keeping stacks of file and heaps of paper at your workplace. Throw what all you don't need. Put important documents in folders. Keep the files in their respective drawers with labels on top of each file. It saves time which goes on unnecessary searching.
- *Don't misuse time*—Do not kill time by loitering or gossiping around. Concentrate on your work and finish assignments on time. Remember your organization is not paying you for playing games on computer or peeping into other's cubicles. First complete your work and then do whatever you feel like doing. Don't wait till the last moment.
- *Be Focused*—One needs to be focused for effective time management.

Develop the habit of using planners, organizers, table top calendars for better time management. Set reminders on phones or your personal computers.

BENEFITS OF TIME MANAGEMENT

Time Management makes an individual punctual and disciplined. One learns to work when it is actually required as a result of effective time management. To make the judicious use of time, individuals should prepare a "TASK PLAN" or a "TO DO" List at the start of the day to jot down activities which need to be done in a particular day as per their importance and urgency against the specific time slots assigned to each activity. A Task Plan gives individuals a sense of direction at the workplace. An individual knows how his day looks like and eventually works accordingly leading to an increased output.

One becomes more organized as a result of effective Time Management. Keeping the things at their proper places minimizes the time which goes on unnecessary searching of documents, important files, folders, stationery items and so on. For better time management, individuals keep their workstations, study zones, cubicles, meeting areas clean and organized. People learn to manage things well as a result of Time Management.

Effective Time Management boosts an individual's morale and makes him confident. As a result of Time Management, individuals accomplish tasks within the stipulated time frame, making them popular in their organization as well as amongst their peers. People who understand the value of time are the ones who manage to stand apart from the crowd. Individuals who finish off work on time are looked up to by others and are always the centre of attention everywhere.

Individuals who stick to a time plan are the ones who realise their goals and objectives within the shortest possible time span. Managing time effectively helps employees to meet targets way ahead of deadlines and finish off task just when it is required.

Effective Time Management helps an employee to reach the pinnacle of success quickly and stay firm at the top for a longer duration. An employee who works just for the sake of working fails to create an impression and is never taken seriously at work. Effective time management plays a pivotal role in increasing an individual's productivity. Output increases substantially when people manage their time well.

Better Time Management helps in better planning and eventually better forecasting. Individuals learn to plan things well and know where exactly they stand five years from now.

Research says that individuals who accomplish tasks on time are less prone to stress and anxiety. Remember there is no point in wasting time and cribbing later. Finish off pending work on time and then you would have ample time for your friends, relatives and family members.

Time Management enables an individual to prioritise tasks and activities at workplace. It is foolish to stay overburdened. Do not accept anything and everything that comes your way.

MAKING TIME MANAGEMENT WORK FOR YOU

Time management is not optional. It is something that everyone who wants to work effectively must consider, whether formally or informally. In fact, virtually everyone practises time management to some degree; the only question is how well they do it and how it affects what they do. Yet, time management is not easy. Nor, even for those who work at it, is it something that anyone gets 100 per cent right. If you think that is a rather ominous start to a book on time management, there is worse to come.

Everyone can benefit from reviewing how to manage their time effectively. In any organization many of the things that actually characterise its very nature make proper time management difficult: hierarchical structures, people, deadlines, paperwork, e-mail, computer problems, meetings, pressures and interactions, both around the organization and externally; all these and more can compound the problems.

The effect of getting to grips with time management can be considerable and varied. It can:

- Affect your efficiency, effectiveness and productivity. This alone makes your attitude to time management very important, for it affects your work day by day, hour by hour, all the time.
- Condition the pressure that goes with any job.
- Create greater positive visibility. Time management is something that will influence how you are perceived by others within the organization. Good time management is an overriding factor that can differentiate people of otherwise equal talent and ability, making it more likely that some will succeed better in career terms than others.

Thus, although it may take some time, getting to grips with your own personal system of time management is immensely important. Time management must be seen as synonymous with self-management; it demands discipline, but discipline reinforced by habit. In other words, the good news is that it gets easier as you work at it. Good habits help ensure a well-organized approach to the way you plan and execute your work.

Making time management work for you is based on two key factors: how you plan your time and how you implement the detail of what you do. The first of these creates an important foundation upon which you can then build and work. The second consists of a multitude of operational factors, practices, methods and tricks, all of which can individually and positively affect the way in which you work. Such factors may be absurdly simple, for example, visibly checking your watch from time to time will tend to make visitors less likely to overstay their welcome, especially if such checks are accompanied by the appropriate look of concern. Or they may demand more complexity, for example, a well-set-up filing system can save time, ensuring that you can locate papers quickly and accurately. Other factors may be downright sneaky, like having a private signal to prompt your secretary to interrupt a meeting with news of something demanding its rapid curtailment or your prompt departure. Furthermore, there is a cumulative effect at work here. This means that the more you adopt or adapt the tricks of the trade that work for you, the more time-efficient you become.

Because of the way time management works, influenced as it is by many things, what works in any particular kind of job or for any particular individual will vary. Some of the ideas you will find presented here, or elsewhere, you will be able to add profitably to your own working habits. Some will be new to you; some you will know but may not be utilizing as effectively as you might. Others will be able to form only the basis of what will suit you.

Be careful not to reject out of hand anything that might be useful in amended form. This is an area where every small influence can assist your overall productivity. Of course, some ideas will not suit you at all. However much you tinker with them, they will not form a useful basis for the kind of way in which you work. What matters is arriving at a point where you are content that, having explored the possibilities for action, you have selected, adapted and experimented with all the methods that can realistically fit in with the way you work and assist your productivity. It is you who matters ultimately, not the principles. However, do remember that anything—but anything—that can help should be considered and, unless it has a negative impact, made part of your working practice. Good time management comes from leaving no stone unturned.

Time may be relative, but it is a resource as valuable as any other. Yet, it is so easy to squander. Why is it that the thought and effort given to the appropriate use of other resources, money for instance, is so much greater than for time? Consider four minutes saved—by not running that mile perhaps. It is easy to think of it as not worthwhile. However, if the four minutes is saved by increasing efficiency on one small task undertaken regularly, then for something done every day that adds up to more than 14 hours over a year! That is very nearly as much as two working days, and should give anyone pause for thought. What could you do—extra—with two additional working days? It is undeniably a useful amount of time and most people have probably got a dozen jobs on their list that could be got out of the way if an additional two days were really available. This thought comes from imagining what speeding up just one small regular task or perhaps avoiding wasting time, to the tune of just four minutes, could do for you. So, another significant reason why time management may be neglected is that individual small savings of time may seem unimportant.

If this fact is recognized, and time and activities planned accordingly, then it is possible to free up considerable amounts of time. What is more, this can often be done at minimal cost. This is worth noting, as many potential improvements to efficiency do have a cost. If you want new equipment, more in your budget, or additional people, then in many organizations this needs considerable justification and may still be turned down. But your time is yours to utilise. It is an area where you can make a real difference to performance armed with little more than the intention to do so.

Yet the principle is clear: there is a time equation that can and must be put to work if time is to be brought under control. There are many ways of ensuring that time is utilized to best effect, and, while some take only a moment, others take time either to set up or for you to adopt the habit of working in a particular way. But beware, because this may only be true at the moment something occurs. Say someone telephones you requesting certain information, imagine also that you must locate and look something up, compose a brief explanatory note and send the information of to the other person. It is a minor matter and will take you three or four minutes. Imagine further that, to avoid the task, you consider letting your secretary do it. Explaining and showing him or her what needs to be done will certainly take 10–15 minutes of your time and your secretary's. It really is quicker to do it yourself. Not so, certainly not if it is a regularly occurring task. If it happens 10 times a week, say, then if you take time to brief your secretary he or she will only have to take it on for less than a week and the time spent briefing will have paid off. Thereafter you save a significant amount of time every week, indeed on every occasion that similar requests are made in the future. This is surely worthwhile. The time equation here of time spent as a ratio of time saved works positively. This is often the case, and allows worthwhile savings to be made, both to simple examples and to more complex matters where hours or days spent on, say, reorganizing a system or process may still pay dividends.

So, why is it so difficult to take this sort of action? Why is the world full of people saying that it is quicker to do some things themselves? Some of the reasons may be to do with attitudes to delegation; beyond that it is largely habit and lack of thought—and perhaps the pressure of the moment. It is worth a thought. Become determined not to be caught in this time trap and you are en route to saving a great deal of time. Given the right intention, and motivation, it is possible for anyone to improve their time utilization, and to do so markedly if you have not thought about it recently. Make no mistake, however, the process does not stop there. The best time managers have not only instilled in themselves good habits and so put part of the process on auto pilot, so to speak, they also view time management as an area of perpetual fine-tuning. In everything they do the time dimension is considered. It becomes a prerequisite for the various ways in which they work. And they continuously strive to improve still further—changing the way they work and what it allows them to achieve. That fine-tuning too becomes a habit.

PERFECT TIMING

Time management is very much an area where the old saying 'Never let perfection be the enemy of the good' is entirely appropriate. However, well you approach the management of your time, you are never going to be able to regard it as perfect. Nothing will guarantee that you will never be unable to find anything again, nor will it mean nothing takes longer in future than you think it will, nor that you are never interrupted again, not least at a crucial moment. But though perfection may not be possible, improvement certainly is. Every saving of time, every productivity gain, whether large or small, adds to the total way in which your style of working contributes to your effectiveness. Any aspect of a job can probably be changed for the better, in terms of how it is done, to use time more productively. This means that you must actively organize what you do and how you do it to produce optimum working and to be really effective. It is this process that using the principles of time management and adopting the right attitude can assist. Doing this and doing it thoroughly will benefit you and your organization; and some of those benefits can come quickly.

It is difficult for an individual to challenge this culture, but it should not be followed slavishly. The ideas of effective time management operate within some definition of the 'working day', and that will vary for every individual just simply adding hours unthinkingly can only achieve so much. The intention here is to show that changing habits and enhancing effectiveness by adopting the right way of working pay dividends. If you do this and achieve your objectives, then maybe the pressure to just 'put in more time' will decrease. If you are managing other people and creating the culture then this aspect may be worth a moment's thought.

2

STEPS OF TIME MANAGEMENT

The judicious use of time by an individual to succeed in all aspects of life refers to *Time Management*. Time Management not only helps individuals to make the best use of time but also ensures successful accomplishment of tasks within the stipulated time frame. It is essential to do the right thing at the right time to earn respect at work. People who do not value time fail to make a mark and are never taken seriously.

Whatever your individual job, whether you are manager or executive, and regardless of the type of organization for which you work and the functional area in which you are involved, you doubtless have many different things to do; too many perhaps. These are different in nature and complexity, and involve different timescales. What is more, you probably have a good many things on the go at once as well as overlapping, perhaps conflicting, priorities. Often work feels just like the jugglingz, and your 'reach'—how much you can keep on the go at once—is an important aspect of your effectiveness. If you exceed your reach then, like the juggler, the danger is that you do not simply drop one torch but several. It helps, when considering managing all of this effectively, to categorise the many elements.

There are doubtless many ways of doing this, but just four categories seem to bring some order to the picture:

1. *Planning.* This is the prerequisite to all action. Many tasks are involved: research, investigation, analysis and testing amongst others. This area may also involve consultation and ultimately the communication of plans and is, of course, the key to decision-making.
2. *Implementation.* Simply stated, doing things—of all sorts—whether intangible (of which the key one is making decisions) or tangible. Specific tasks divide into two sorts. First, individual tasks. These are freestanding. They may be major or minor. For example, a writing task may entail composing a two-line e-mail or a 20-page report. Second, progressing tasks where a series of closely linked actions contribute cumulatively to achieving an overall result. Moving offices would involve such actions and such things may be more clearly visualized rather than described—indeed flowcharts provide a useful and time-efficient way of working on them. Tasks in both categories may well need to be linked to planning activity on whatever scale.
3. *Monitoring and control.* Checking may well be necessary to ensure things are being done in the best possible way and bringing the desired results. Checking may be simple, editing the draft of a report or running it through the spellchecker, for example. Or it may be complex, as are many financial control systems.
4. *Communicating and dealing with people.* This clearly overlaps with the other three categories of activity, but is inherent in the work of almost everyone. Few, if any, people work in isolation from others,

and for most, the people issues, whether it is briefing them or reporting to them, meetings and other forms of communication with them, are an essential part of their work and take up a major part of their time.

In all four categories, there will or should be a strong link with objectives and achievement of results. All tasks and all actions should focus on the overall aims and are often of little significance in themselves. Effectiveness is measured ultimately by achievement. Time management must not be seen as only concerned with packing more activity into the available time, though this may be part of it; it must be instrumental in ensuring that objectives are met. It may be a cliché, but it must not be forgotten that activity must never be confuzed with achievement.

ASSESS YOUR WORKING PRACTICE

You may think that you know how you work; perhaps you feel you know all too well—warts and all. But do not be misled into thinking that considering in detail how you do things is a waste of time. Classically, improving anything implies the identification of how it is now. Further, such an analysis can provide valuable information about where the greatest improvement may be found, all of which makes improvement more likely. This is certainly true of time management, more so perhaps because this is an area where there is a real tendency to self-delusion. You are no doubt essentially efficient, but improvement may still be possible. Indeed, most people would value more time to complete their tasks and undertake their responsibilities, if this were possible. To make other than superficial changes, you need to know something about your own working practices and pressures, and where time goes at present. In a complex job, many activities are involved.

Where Time Goes?

There are two ways to consider this. The first is to estimate it, guesstimate if necessary. This is most easily done in percentage terms on a pie chart.

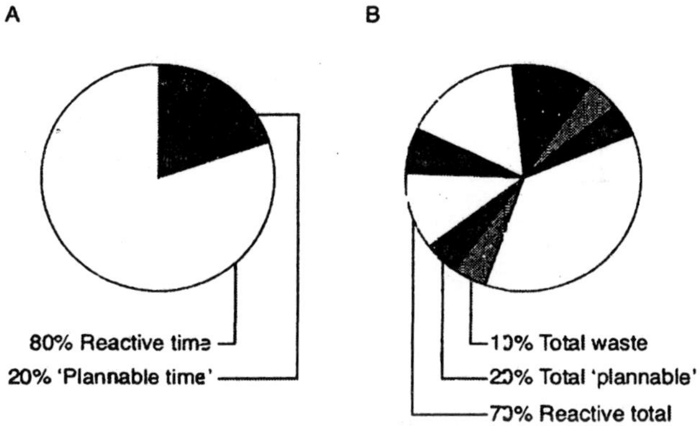

Figure 1

The second is to use a time log to obtain a much more accurate picture—literally recording what you do through the day and doing so for at least a week, longer if you can.

Few people keep a log without surprising themselves, and the surprises can be either that much more time is spent in some areas than you think, or that certain things take up less time than you think—mainly the former. Some obvious areas for review usually come to mind as a result.

Again using the simple pie chart, it can be useful as a second stage of this review to list what you would ideally like the time breakdown to be. This puts a clear picture in your mind of what you are working towards. Such a picture might even be worth setting out before you read on. All this gives you something to aim towards and will tell you progressively – as you take action – whether that action is having a positive effect.

Name:..................................Comments::..................................
Date::..................................

No.	Start time	Activity description	Time taken (minutes)	Priority* category A B C D	Comments
1					
2					
3					
4					
5					
6					
7					
8					
9					
10					
11					
12					
13					
14					
15					
16					
17					
18					
19					
20					
21					
22					
23					

*Link these columns to any priority code you use

Total time taken (minutes):

Figure 2. Personal time performance log (example)

If all the remaining review points are looked at alongside this information then you can see more clearly whether you are able to take action to improve things, and whether the points refer to areas that are critical for you. With all this in mind, we turn to what is both one of the basics of time management and perhaps its most practically important tenet.

PLAN THE WORK

Certainly any real progress with time management needs a plan. This must be in writing and must be reviewed and updated regularly; for most people this means a daily check. Not only is it updated regularly, it provides a snapshot of your workload ahead at any particular moment. As such it should show accurately and completely your work plan for the immediate future, and give an idea of what lies beyond. As you look ahead there will be some things that are clear, for example when an annual budget must be prepared and submitted. Other areas are less clear and, of course, much cannot be anticipated at all in advance. At its simplest, such a plan is just a list of things to do. It may include:

- a daily plan;
- a weekly plan;
- commitments that occur regularly (weekly or monthly or annually);
- a plan for the coming month (perhaps linked to a planning chart).

The exact configuration will depend on the time span across which you work. What is important is that it works for you, that it is clear, that different kinds of activity show up for what they are and that it links clearly to your diary and appointment system. How such a list is arranged and how you can use it to improve your work and effectiveness are important, but the fact of the system and the thinking that its regular review prompts are also important in their own right. It is the basic factor in creating a time management discipline, and it provides much of the information from which you must make choices—what you do, delegate, delay or ignore, in what order you tackle things and so on. Good time management does not remove the need to make decisions of this sort, but it should make them easier and quicker to make and it should enable you to make decisions that really do help in a positive way, so that you get more done and in the best way to achieve your aims..

CONTROLLING THE UNCONTROLLABLE

A final point here is crucial. Some people, perhaps most, have a measure of their day that is reactive. Things occur that cannot be predicted, at least individually, and a proportion of the available time is always going to go in this way. Such activity is not automatically unimportant, and the reverse may well be true. For example, a manager on the sales or marketing side of a commercial company may have enquiries and queries coming from customers that are very important and must be dealt with promptly, but will nevertheless make fitting in everything else more difficult. Sometimes the reaction to this is to believe that, because of this reactive element, it is not possible to plan or to plan effectively. The reverse is true. If your days do consist, even in part, of this sort of random activity, it is even more important to plan because there is inherently less time available to do the other things that the job involves and that time has to be planned even more thoroughly to maximize its effectiveness. Everyone needs a plan and everyone can benefit from having a clear view of what there is to be done. If you do not have this then the work of setting it up will take a moment, but it is worthwhile and it need not then take long to keep up to date. Once it is in place, you can evolve a system that suits you and that keeps up with the way in which your job and its responsibilities change over time.

TIME MANAGEMENT SYSTEM

Many books on the subject of time management are closely linked to some specific proprietary time management system, consisting of diaries, flies, binders and so on. Some even claim that the only route to time efficiency lies with their particular system.

Many are restrictive, that is, they can only be used in a particular way and that may well not suit you and the way you think and work. There is thus a real danger that if you use a system and some element of it does not work for you, then your use of the whole system falters. A better way is perhaps to work out what you need first, asking:

- What kind of diary do need?
- How much space do need for notes?
- How many sections fit the way my tasks are grouped?
- What permanent filing is necessary? etc.

Then, when you have thought through what you need and worked that way for a while (a process that will almost certainly have you making a few changes in the light of how things actually work), you can check out the systems and see whether any of them formalise what you want to do and, as they can be expensive, make the investment worthwhile. Otherwise, many people organize themselves perfectly well with no more than a diary, a notebook or a file. After all, it must reflect your plan and it is your time that you want to organize. Of course, another option these days is to go electronic, so any form may be on screen rather than paper; but the same thinking applies to selecting what is best.

SETTING CLEAR OBJECTIVES

Any plan is only as good as the objectives that lie behind it. Clear objectives really are important, and any lack of clarity can affect every aspect of a person's work, not least time management, sometimes doing so surreptitiously.

SMART Objectives

Maxims advocating setting clear objectives are everywhere; they offer sound advice. You do need clear objectives, and they must not be vague or general hopes. A much quoted acronym spells out the principles involved: objectives should be SMART, that is: Specific, Measurable, Achievable, Realistic, and Timed.

It is all too easy to define the objectives for a workshop on this topic as being simply to ensure participants 'make better presentations', a statement that is unlikely to be sufficiently clear to be really useful. Objectives for a presentation skills course should be:

- *Specific.* To enable participants to make future presentations in a manner and style that will be seen as appropriate by their respective audiences, and which will enhance the message they put over.
- *Measurable.* In other words, how will we know this has been achieved? Ultimately, in this case, by the results of future presentations; but we might also consider that the trainer or the group, or both, will be able to judge this to a degree at the end of the event by observing the standard during practice.
- *Achievable.* Can this be done? The answer in this case will depend on the prevailing standard before

the course. If the people are inexperienced and their standard of presentation is low, then the answer may be that it cannot.

- *Realistic.* Picking up the last point, if the time is, say, inadequate then the objectives may not be realistic. Potentially, these people can be improved, we might say, but not in one short session.
- *Timed.* In training terms, this will reflect the timing of the course. It may be scheduled to take place in one month's time, so the objectives cannot be realized before then. Also consider the duration: is a one, two or any other number of days' programme going to do the job?

Much of what needs to be done to manage time effectively is concerned with tackling conflicts and making decisions about what comes first, and none of this is possible if there is no underlying clarity about objectives to act as a reference.

This is not the place for a long treatise on objective setting. Suffice it to say that this is important to everything in corporate life. A company functions best with clear corporate objectives, the management structure works best when individuals are clear about what it is they are expected to achieve. Consider your own position. Are there any areas that are not clear in this respect? Do objectives make for problems or conflict regarding the way you go about the job? If you answered 'yes' to the first question, then you probably did the same for the second.

Note: you will never be a good time manager unless you have clear objectives as part of your overall job description. If you do not, this is something you must seek to resolve. If you have an idea of where time goes now and how you really approach things, if you have a plan—relating clearly to your job objectives—then you can get to work with some hopes of being reasonably productive. But there are many factors that can work to increase that productivity. Some are not only fundamental, but are also good examples of the way in which approaches (ultimately habits) can exert a considerable and ongoing influence on your working practices. The examples that follow are all potentially of great value to the manager wanting to become truly time-efficient.

THINKING AHEAD

This might appropriately be called the opposite of the 'if only...' school of ineffective time management. Too often people find themselves in a crisis, the resolution of which would be all too easy if we could wind the clocks back. In all honesty, though the unexpected can happen sometimes, crisis management is all too common, and often all too unnecessary. Coping well with crises saves time—certainly if the alternative is panic.

Don't Panic

Whatever the cause and implications of any crisis situation, the rule has to be 'Never treat a crisis like a crisis.' Panic implies an absence of all the usual management processes that are no less needed at such a time; perhaps they are needed in fuller measure than usual. Having a systematic approach in mind (and acquiring the habit of referring to it, albeit mentally) as a first conscious step to avoiding panic is useful. Blind, unthinking action will rarely have the precision required to rescue the situation and more damage may be done—and more time wasted—as further second-stage action becomes necessary. So, the rules are:

- Stay cool and do not panic.

- Think (and what is more, take sufficient time to think straight).
- Consider the full range of management skills that could sort out the situation (this may include simple tactics such as delegating certain straightforward actions to give you time to resolve more complex issues, and more radical solutions, such as reviewing policy).
- Make an action plan (especially important if there is any degree of complexity involved).
- Consider the control aspect of that ongoing action plan (simplistically creating a mechanism to show progress and let you know when the crisis is past).

Then considered action can systematically sort out the problem, at least as best as possible—you cannot wind the clock back. Finally, attention can turn not only to the lessons to be learnt (so as not to repeat similar disasters), but also to anything positive that might come from the whole incident. Think positive. The Chinese ideogram for crisis consists of two characters: the first one means 'severe danger', the second means 'opportunity'. Enough said. Thereafter, you need to keep things in proportion. A crisis may impose stresses and strains, and surviving the occasional one is part of most jobs—though working so that they do not occur is perhaps even more important. As Anton Chekhov said, 'Any idiot can face a crisis—it's the day to day living that wears you out.'

If things are left late or ill-thought out (the two often go together), then time is used up in a hasty attempt to sort things out at short notice. This tends to make any task more difficult and is compounded by whatever day-to-day responsibilities are current at the time. If you can acquire the habit of thinking ahead—a system, as referred to above, will help you do this—then you are that much more likely to see when a start really needs to be made on something. Some people find that to 'see' the pattern of future work and tasks in their mind's eye is difficult. One invaluable aid to this is the planning or wall chart. This enables you to create a picture of activities, and the time spans are very much clearer as you scan such a chart than when ficking through the pages of a diary. Charts come in all shapes and sizes; some are for the current year and are, effectively, large diaries; others are ruled for specific tasks, and others still are designed for you to create the detail.

SAVE TIME

Whatever actions you might consider taking to keep yourself well organized—and there are many—they tend to fall into two categories: ones simple to implement, that only take a moment, and those that inherently take some time to set up, and perhaps some time thereafter to acquire as a retained working habit. If you limit yourself to the former, you will never maximize your time management effectiveness. So, returning to an earlier example, that of saying 'It's quicker to do it myself', in the short term the sentiment is often correct. It is quicker for you to do it, but this is only true at the moment something occurs. Suffice it to say that this is an area that needs to become a sort of reflex. Every time you find yourself taking action based on this premise, stop and think for a moment whether you are doing the right thing. Is there a longer-term route that would be more useful? The more you do this, the more time you will save and the more you will be able to do it. There is a virtuous circle here. It stands some thought. Become determined not to be caught in the trap implicit here, and you are on a track that will save you a great deal of time in future.

TAKING TIME TO THINK

At the end of the training film Time to Think, the main character, a manager who has come to grips with managing his time better, is sitting in his office. A colleague comes into the outer office and begins to walk past the secretary to see him. The secretary stops him, says her manager is busy and suggests he makes an appointment to see him later. He looks past her at the manager sitting in his office and says: 'But he's not doing anything...' Immediately the secretary replies that: 'He's thinking; now do you want to see him this afternoon or...' This incident makes a good point.

As a general rule it is true to say that the higher up the hierarchy of an organization you go, you are expected to spend more time thinking, planning and decision making and less doing other things. It is also often true that the thinking, the planning and the idea generation that goes into a job are usually the most important things to be done in that job. And what is the most difficult kind of time to keep clear and have sufficient of? Time to think will rank high. Make no mistake: many jobs demand a degree of creativity and this is something that is as important to a small change of approach or system as it is to some more radical development.

Giving yourself more time to think creatively, both alone and within a team, may be one of the most important things effective time management can do for you. Go back to your analysis of your time, or better still your time log if you did one and see how these activities show up. Are they getting the time they need and deserve or are they squeezed out by other pressures and the things that are more obviously urgent? Make sure that you set your sights on creating sufficient thinking time—perhaps above all—and that the action you take to achieve this is not offset by unnecessary crises. Without something approaching the ideal in this area, all your objectives may be in jeopardy.

BE PREPARED TO SAY 'NO'

This is very much a first principle, and it needs some resolve to carry it through. Everyone has to accept that they cannot do everything. This must be taken literally because there may be an almost infinite amount to do in any job that has some kind of inherent innovative or creative nature to it. Many people could just go on listing more and more things to do, not all equally important but deserving of a place on their 'To do' list nevertheless. Even if your job is not like this, you certainly have to accept that you are not going to do everything when you want. Both in terms of quantity and priority you are going to have to say 'no' to some things. It is worth considering here not so much what you leave out but whom you say 'no' to. For instance, you may have to turn down:

- *Colleagues.* What is involved here can vary and if there is a network of favours, with everyone helping everyone else, you do not want to let it get out of hand either way. Turn down too much and you end up losing time because people are reluctant to help you. Do everything unquestioningly and you may be seen as a soft touch and will end up doing more than your share. So balance and timing are the keynotes here; you do not have to do everything that crops up in this way instantly.
- *Subordinates.* Here they cannot tell you to do things, and while they need support, this must not get out of hand.
- *Your own boss.* Working with a boss who does not have enough to do, or who expects everything to

be done instantly just because he or she is the boss, can play havoc with the best intentions of time management. You may need to regard it as your mission to educate your boss and need to conduct a campaign of persuasion and negotiation to keep any unreasonable load down.

With all of these you need to resolve to think before you agree, and to turn down some potential involvements even though they might be attractive to you. But this is not all; the most difficult person to say 'no' to may well be yourself. There are always many reasons for saying 'yes' to things: you do not wish to offend others, you want to do whatever it is, you do not think about the way a new thing impinges on the current workload, etc. It was well put by Charles Spurgeon: 'Learn to say no; it will be more use to you than to be able to read Latin.'

TO BE, OR NOT TO BE

There is, however, a dichotomy here, one well summed up in a quotation from Robert Heimleur, who said: 'They didn't want it good, they wanted it on Wednesday.' The fact is it takes time to achieve perfection, and in any case, perfection may not always be strictly necessary. This comes hard to those who are naturally perfectionists, and it is a trait that many have at least about some things, but it is necessary to strike a balance. The key balance to be struck is between quality—the standard to which things are done—and cost and time. It is one that needs to be consciously struck.

There is always a trade-of here, and it is not always the easiest thing to achieve. Often a real compromise has to be made. Cost is often key in this. It would be easy to achieve the quality of output you want in many things, but only if cost were no object. And in most jobs, budget considerations rank high. It is useful to get into the way of thinking about things in these terms, and doing so realistically so that you consider what is necessary as well as what is simply desirable or ideal. In doing this there is one key factor that needs to be built in: a significant cost is your time.

For some, this is easy to cost. People like accountants or consultants will charge for their time by the day or hour and this makes them sensitive to just what costs are involved. In an organization it is not just a question of dividing your salary to produce an hourly cost; you have to allow the many other costs of your being there. Factors will include everything from your office and office supplies to the cost of support—your secretary, for example, if you have one—and, of course, the cost of other benefits you receive in addition to salary.

It is worth your making this kind of calculation; the resultant figure may surprise you and it is a useful benchmark when considering many things in managing your time—whether you should make a journey, hold or attend a meeting and so on. Otherwise make sure you always keep in mind the balance to be struck between quality, cost and time. If you do not over-engineer quality seeking a standard that is not in some instances necessary or desirable, then you will surely save time.

WORK SMARTER NOT LONGER

The answer to productivity in your job is not to work longer and longer hours. This may seem like a contradiction in terms. Surely if you put in more hours you will achieve more as a result? Yes, of course the direct answer to that is that you will. The point, however, is that there are limits.

After all, you get out what you put in and working hard must make a difference. But it is here that another balance must be struck for most people: that between work and home and outside interests and commitments. If you overdo the work, the other things—and they are all important—suffer. What is more, damage, if damage is done, is insidious. You may not be aware of a difficulty until it is too late and begins to cause some real problems. The answer is to seek to strike a balance; indeed, you may want to lay down some rules for yourself about this, specifying maximum hours to work, travel or spend on specific things. In addition, for those readers who are managers, remember that the work capacity of the team you control is very much greater than yours, so it always makes sense to take a team view of things rather than just opting to do more yourself. Finally, excessively long hours worked can be misunderstood and make it appear to others that you are inefficient, which is presumably the reverse of how you want to appear. Long hours will be necessary on some occasions, to complete a particular project, say, but in excess are likely to produce declining standards and run risks that make working smarter a much more attractive option. It is something to ponder in order to make sure that you create a working pattern that is well balanced in this way.

REWARD YOURSELF

It has already been said that time management is not easy, that it demands a concerted effort, so you need to motivate yourself and give yourself some real reasons to make it work. You need something more than just getting to the bottom of your in-tray. In any case, even the most effective person may never do this and, while what you achieve and how that is received is reward enough in some ways, what is wanted is something that is linked more specifically to your own success in managing your time. It thus makes sense to set yourself specific time management goals and to link them to what that will do for you; to give yourself personal satisfaction so that you are very aware that succeeding in what you intend in time terms will make something else possible. Such rewards may be seemingly small and personal, but nevertheless an example may make the point.

If you can think in this kind of way and give yourself some sort of reward—better still a number of them—then your attention will remain focused on what time management can do for you. A major outcome of good time manager is the ability to fit in projects that might otherwise be delayed, curtailed or omitted. Make such a pet project your reward, work out what is necessary in other areas to achieve it and you are just that much more likely to achieve what you want. Everything reviewed so far will help you create a better basis for becoming more efficient Time Manager. In particular it will help you to adopt the right attitudes in terms of the overall approach to your work, and in terms of specific areas of activity. In real life, good intentions have a habit of deserting you at particular moments in favour of expediency—or panic! It may be easier to adopt a trigger to memory rather than a more all-embracing intention. Saying that you will say 'no' to more requests may be difficult to apply consistently. However, some people find that resolving to count from 1 to 10 before accepting unwelcome and avoidable requests without due consideration does work. Rather than being rushed into a 'yes', they are able to give a considered response, perhaps one that has the intention of avoiding the involvement. Of course, nothing like this is infallible. However, if such a ploy reduces this kind of acceptance in any sort of worthwhile way, then it is useful, and other areas may be susceptible to similar thinking.

❖❖❖

3

SETTING DEADLINE

Time management helps an individual to make the best possible use of time. It is essential for individuals to value time and allocate the right time to the right activity. Organization and time management go together. Being well organized creates the right time environment. Poor organization is insidious; everything takes just a little bit more time than it should and this adds up day by day, inevitably reducing effectiveness. This is true of even minor faults or omissions which, duplicated across a number of activities, can together have a significant effect and dilute efficiency. At worst, a lack of organization causes real, even debilitating, problems.

A poorly organized person:

- cannot locate papers and information easily;
- allows muddle to enter their diary, sometimes to the point of double-booking;
- is inclined to 'task hop', moving between tasks in an attempt to meet many and conflicting deadlines, completing things erratically;
- is late and ill-prepared for meetings;
- allows paperwork to proliferate;
- has no clear priorities;

- works in a mess;
- communicates poorly and keeps inadequate records.

As a result, they end up duplicating effort, wasting time, missing deadlines, and delivering inadequate or insufficient results, even after having apparently put in the time and effort required. Worse still in some ways, such poor performance is both visible to, and affects, others. Colleagues whose work overlaps with such a person are inconvenienced, the perpetrator collects a reputation for unreliability and not only is work affected but so are things such as personal promotion prospects. It is all very well to stress the disadvantages of being disorganized, but how do you get, and stay, organized? Some are simple ideas, though they can have a significant influence nevertheless. Others are more fundamental. All perhaps need some thought to fit them to your existing methods of working, but many can also readily become habits so that you stop wasting time thinking about their implementation.

WORK THE PLAN

There is more to this than just recording a list of 'Things to do'. Tasks must be noted in the right kind of way and the way you review the list can usefully follow a pattern. One such is the so-called LEAD system, with the letters of the word 'lead' standing for:

- *List the activities*. This must be done comprehensively, though in note form as you do not want the list to become unmanageable.
- *Estimate* how long each item will take, as accurately as possible.
- *Allow time for contingency* as things always have a potential for taking longer than your best estimate;

also allow time for regular tasks, the ongoing things that go on as a routine day by day.

- *Decide priorities.* This is a key, and one of the most important aspects of time management for anyone.

Scan the plan, reviewing it overall probably once a day. This process should become a routine. What other action may be necessary will depend on the pattern of your day and work. Something cropping up during the day may be either thought about and added to the list at the time or simply put on one side to be incorporated into the plan at the next review. Proprietary systems set it out in particular ways, sectioning things and arranging them under headings; and if this helps that is fine, but many find their own simpler system works perfectly well. A sheet ruled into a number of spaces or the use of a second colour, or both, can make what may well be a full list easier to follow. If items are reliably listed and the list conscientiously reviewed then you will keep on top of things and certainly nothing should be forgotten.

BATCH YOUR TASKS

The trouble with so many jobs is that the list of things to do is itself apt to get unmanageable—unless the tasks are batched. An overriding principle of good time management is to batch your tasks. Here again the proprietary systems all have their own methodology, but what works best for you is the only measure. It does not matter too much what you call them:

- Priority
- Important
- Action now
- Obtain more information
- Reading.

These are some of the options (and there are those who manage perfectly well with A, B and C). You will also need File and may consider other action categories such as Telephone, Write, Discuss (perhaps divided into categories such as e-mails or reports), and similar ones that are particular to your business and your role in it, such as Proposals, Quotations and the names of products, departments or systems. The important thing at this stage is to work out how many and what titles of batches suit you, and that this and the way you arrange your desk are not in conflict. A manageable number of batches of this sort can, if you wish, link physically to filing trays on your desk or some distinguishing mark on flies themselves. One grouping, which can logically be commented on at this point, is events, most often appointments, which routine use of a diary can automatically batch together.

USE YOUR DIARY EFFECTIVELY

A good clear diary system is a must. Many formal systems combine the conventional diary with their sophisticated version of the 'Things to do' list. One thing that certainly works well, and which a loose-leaf system allows, is to have at one opening of a binder a convenient complete picture of your day, showing both appointments and things to do. Confusion is caused in many offices over what constitutes the master diary. A desk diary often lives on the secretary's desk, another in the executive's pocket and sometimes there is more duplication such as with a wall planner or computer system. This needs to be clear, and where appropriate, necessitates regular updates between the executive and the secretary, who must clearly both communicate and have an understanding about who does what. Small things have an effect on efficiency. The diary should:

- Be with you everywhere, everyday.
- Be placed next to you on your desk open to the relevant day or week.
- Show full details, certainly full enough to be clear.
- Show how long is set aside for things.
- Be completed in pencil so that alterations can be made without creating an illegible mess.

Writing diary is simple but effective way to develop and enhance understanding about yourself, understanding about how you become what you are, what directions you want to go ahead in your life.

A planner element within a diary is very useful. Perhaps the most important difference between just an appointments diary and a time management system is if it is used to schedule all of the working time rather than just appointments. The two additions are: tasks, actually setting aside time to work on a specific project, and thinking time, so that planning and creative work is not carried out, as so often happens, only in gaps that are left between appointments and meetings. If this is done—leaving some space for the unexpected and any reactive part of the work, and linked to the concept of the rolling plan, you will stay much more organized and better able to judge how things are progressing, whether deadlines will be met and tasks completed. Two final points. The diary is a vital tool, to be guarded and treated with respect. It is also, therefore, a good place to keep other key information, telephone numbers and other data you need at your fingertips, provided you do not overburden it so that it becomes too thick and unmanageable.

The computer, and a variety of electronic personal organizers, are taking over some of these activities. Often this works well. Being able to set a meeting with six colleagues, some in different cities, at the touch of a button on a networked system may well save time. But for many people a personal diary or planner, usable anywhere there is a pencil, will always be a part of what helps them work effectively. Certainly, the thinking that needs to be applied to diary organization is the same however the information involved may be recorded.

SCHEDULE APPOINTMENTS WITH CARE

Appointments, transactions with other people, take up a major amount of many executives' time. Exactly when you programme them makes a real difference to your productivity. Allow sufficient time; one appointment running into another always causes problems. And always schedule a period of time, in other words, a finishing time as well as a start time. It is impossible to do this with 100 per cent accuracy, but it helps. Think about:

- The potential for interruptions.
- The location. A meeting room may be better than your office, especially if you need to move what you are working on just before it starts.
- Timing that makes it inevitable that it continues into lunch or a drink at the end of the day.
- Timing that restricts your ability to schedule other appointments, in the way that something mid-morning could mean there is not sufficient time to fit in another meeting before it, or after it and before lunch.

And take especial care with gatherings that involve more than one person. You have to be accommodating here, but do not always consider others' convenience before your own—it is you who will suffer. Always record appointments clearly in the diary. While considering when to schedule appointments, it may be worth a slight digression to make a point about the most fundamental level of scheduling: that affected by your personal time clock. Accommodating your nature in this respect is one of many areas where you will never achieve perfection, but that is no reason to ignore it; get things mostly right and you will be more productive and waste less time.

CLEAR YOUR DESK

They mean it too and some of them are right. But, and it is a big but, this kind of disorder rarely goes with good time management. It pays to be neat. It pays you and it may also pay the organization for which you work. This is worth another slight digression. If you are employed by a large organization, you are not indispensable. Sorry, but it is true. What is more, it is incumbent in your responsibilities that you protect the continuity of operations and this includes thinking about what happens if you are, for any reason, not there. Even a short absence by someone on sick leave, say, can cause havoc. It takes others a while to locate things you were working on and, because of the difficulty, matters can be disrupted or delayed. Worse perhaps from your point of view, when you return and other people have been rifing through your system, you are not going to be able to find anything. So resolve to keep your desk tidy. This means having a clear, and clearly labelled, system, one that is likely to be more specific than an 'In' and 'Out' tray and is reasonably intelligible to others. This can be accommodated in part by your diary and planning system, which can link to and identify where things are—in flies or whatever—but still the need is there.

AVOID 'CHERRY PICKING'

Your approach to time management needs to be systematic. Some of the techniques that have been discussed here demand habit and a consistent approach. Some people are good at this, they make the plan, they list the priorities, they have a good diary and time system and are careful about their decisions and work practice in terms of how they affect the way they use time. But they then make one significant mistake that negates all this effort: they cherry pick. That is, they keep picking out jobs, possibly for one of the reasons that was reviewed earlier, such as because they like them. Whatever the reason, they keep rethinking their priorities and deciding that something else must be done first. They can spend so much time doing this that the plan never settles and time is not spent primarily actioning it. Of course, a time plan is not static. It does need regular fine-tuning, but this must not become an excuse for not sticking to it. If your plan is reviewed regularly, and if the decisions made about it are good ones, then you can stick to it and will make more progress through the work list by doing so. Have confidence in your plan and resist being sidetracked by anything and it will work better for you.

USE ABSTRACTS

No one needs reminding of the amount of reading there is to do in most jobs. For some it is very important to keep up to date with the technical area their job involves, for others management processes themselves are worth regular study. In both cases, the first task is to decide which, from the very many references published, should command your attention. This first selection exercise can be time-consuming in itself before you actually study anything individually.

If the thought of this facility appeals to you then you may want to check locally what services are available. Typically, they will come from libraries, colleges, trade associations and professional bodies, business schools and the like. Many can now be delivered by e-mail. If you find something that offers a service that appears to suit you then it is perhaps worth taking out a subscription for a short period and see whether it does save you time. If it does, and if it also helps you find information you might otherwise miss, it can then be economic to continue, in which case you have another continuing time saver on your side.

THE INTERNET

The internet provides a source of almost infinite information, one that can be accessed quickly and, once mastered, easily. And this can be done at minimal cost without leaving your workplace.

Beware, however, surfing the internet is a major source of distraction. One thing leads all too easily to another and it can be tempting to spend a minute or two more 'just in case you can access something better or more specific', and then a minute or two more again. Be warned, some real discipline may be necessary here—for yourself and perhaps on behalf of others whom you manage. Note: another new word has entered the language: cyberloafing. Not only is a vast amount of time wasted by people surfing the internet in ways that have nothing to do with work, some of it is so inappropriate that it has become grounds for dismissal. Avoid it; and resist too the social pressure involved in circulating jokes and other material by e-mail.

INSIST ON QUALITY

Quality has always mattered, and always will, but is currently enjoying something of a special emphasis with Quality Management having been elevated into a major issue, often under the name Total Quality Management. This is no bad thing as anything that emphasizes so important an aspect of corporate performance is all to the good. Look at this for a moment on a more local scale. Consider your office, your department. Does it do a good job? Now you may well answer, 'Of course', but how do you really know? Ask: Are there sufficient performance standards? Are you aiming specifically at achieving particular levels in all activities? And so on.

For example, in the area of customer service, a bank may specify that no more than three customers should be in a single queue, that each should receive a greeting as they are attended to and that the customer's name should be used at the end of the transaction as they depart. Small points perhaps, but it is the summation of such points that add up to the standard of customer service that they intend to provide. Such standards are designed not simply to specify what should happen, but to make it more certain that the standards are achieved in practice. You may have noticed how much time is sometimes spent sorting out things that have gone wrong. And this need not mean very wrong, but just falling short of the ideal by a small margin. Consider the bank example again. If customers are kept waiting just a little too long some of them will comment on the fact, the cashier will apologise and perhaps explain, and the transaction will then proceed, usually without further problem. But it will take a little longer than it would otherwise, and with many hundreds of people seen each day at the counter this matters, not least to other customers whose wait is increased.

This is a simple example, but similar things will apply in your office. If you and your team get things right, and know what is necessary to get it right, then things will take less time, first because tasks will be performed efficiently, second because there will be less time wasted in any disruption caused by performance to a lesser standard. Quality is a great friend of good time management. You should think about the standards of work with which you are involved, and clarify this area if necessary. Further, if there are moves within your organization to embrace the likes of Total Quality Management, this will be worth supporting. There are set-up costs and time needs to be invested also, but the equation is likely to work. Such initiatives will save time. 'Do it right and the time it takes will be less' is a good general principle and can be applied to many areas of work. Quality saves time.

ACTION OR INVESTMENT

Few people are bad time managers because they are idle. Certainly most of those with an interest in time management are busy people, but they are not getting everything done, or everything done thoroughly and on time. And the thing that gets neglected most is investment time; this is time taken now to ensure improvements or results in future—the planning and analysis and other such activities necessary to make progress in any area. Categorizing on your plan which category of time you are scheduling will help create a balance. Thus the plan will show whether time is to be taken up with people (appointments, meetings, etc.) or tasks. It will also allow for the unexpected. And this will be seen at a glance, maybe in the double opening of a loose-leaf book, so that fine-tuning can take place if necessary.

If you have a good feel for how much of your job should be spent in action time and how much in investment time, then you will be better able to maintain the balance you need, using the techniques of time management to create the working pattern you want. Time management is, and should be regarded as, a personal tool, something that you use to help you and not a standard approach that you must adopt in order to be efficient.

A GOOD PERSONAL ASSISTANT

There is an old story told about a secretary to a much-travelling and very senior executive. Asked by someone one day if he could see him, she replied that she was sorry but he was in Singapore. 'Abroad again', he replied, 'He's always overseas. Tell me, who does all his work while he's away?' She looked him straight in the eye and answered without hesitation: 'The same person who does it when he's here.' Some personal assistants or secretaries perhaps have such authority, but while they are a panacea no more than the time management system sold on the basis that it will reorganize your life effortlessly is, he or she can help. For those who have one, a good PA can be not only the recipient of some of your delegation, he or she can also act as a regular prompt to good time management and take a genuinely active role in organizing you, or your whole department.

The characteristics of the ideal PA are many and varied. As well as typing, and sometimes shorthand, skills, he or she must be familiar with an increasing array of office technology. But what of time management? Whether a person has a natural or acquired organizational ability is difficult to assess at an interview, as is whether he or she really cares about such things. If you can do so, however, and only appoint a candidate who has characteristics of this sort, then you will have a real asset on board in your battle to win the time war. Ask any questions you can think of that will give you information in this area, particularly about past experience in managing the diary and appointments of previous employers. This is also something to check when taking up references; it is always worth doing in almost any recruitment situation. At this level, a phone call—with the permission of the candidate—to a last employer is probably the quickest check. It will be likely to give the best information anyway as people are reluctant to take the time or make the commitment to put references in writing.

There are two other important characteristics in a PA that you should seek. First, the ability to work your way. This is important as there may be existing procedures and systems, as well as management style, that you need your PA to fit in with; on the other hand, always be ready to learn from him or her. There is no monopoly on good ideas, and in this area you should be on the look out for ideas from any source, the only criterion being that the ideas are useful. A good PA will also have sufficient 'weight' or clout, that is, he or she must be able to stand up for you with colleagues and others, to say 'no' on your behalf and to make requests on your behalf—and make it stick. Achieve this and your attempts to control your time will have a permanent ally, one who will work with you to achieve what you want and who will, at best and with experience, take an active role in the process.

COMMUNICATE WITH YOUR PERSONAL ASSISTANT

It is no use having a good PA, one who is sympathetic to time management, and then not communicating with him or her. This is a classic example of something for which there is 'never time' but which, if you do find the time for it, will help you save much more time than this communication takes. Many executives start the day with a meeting with their PA, perhaps when the mail arrives in the morning. You must decide what suits you best and also work out a way of keeping in touch and up to date with your PA if you spend much time out of the office, though modern communications make this easier than once was the case.

Your PA must know how you work and what you have on the go at any particular time. And he or she should, if possible, share your view of priorities, knowing what you are prepared to be interrupted for, which things and people rate most time and attention, and what must be actioned first. Once a PA has some experience, more may well be possible. He or she can take the initiative on things, accompany you to certain meetings and ultimately run whole areas of your office life in a way that improves your utilization of time dramatically. Find areas of real responsibility, let him or her look after them and make the decisions affecting them and it can pay dividends. You must make it work. It is no good coming back to the office after a trip and complaining that things have not been completed or that you now have a string of time-wasting meetings in your diary, if your lack of communication has caused this situation. So, communicate clearly and regularly, and remember that this includes listening. A good relationship does not just happen, it demands some time up front—but the results can be very worthwhile.

USE A 'DOCUMENT PARKING' SYSTEM

This point might equally have been listed under paperwork, but it is so useful a device that it deserves to come in here. Perhaps the best explanation begins with the problem it solves. Many of them do not need action, or cannot be actioned immediately. This is what so often constitutes the ever-present overloaded Pending Tray. The net result is that you spend a great deal of time either shuffling through the heap to locate things, or checking things in there to see what you might, in time, do about them. The nature of some of the material makes the problem worse. Say one item can only be actioned when certain monthly performance figures are published at the end of the month, then to keep checking it may well be both time-consuming and useless as no action can be taken anyway.

Further, constant reviewing can achieve little in advance of knowledge of the figures.

If you suffer this sort of situation you need a parking place for such things, somewhere safe yet guaranteed to trigger prompt action at the appropriate moment. You need what is called a Prompt File. This means you take an item and decide when you will be able to progress it. This may be at a specific time or it may not. Then you simply mark it with the date on which you next want to see it and file it, with other similar items, in date order. Then forget it. Waste no more time even thinking about it. You do not have to, because every day your PA will check the file and bring anything marked with that day's date in to you with the morning mail. At which point you can either act or, occasionally, give it another date and move it forward. A couple of provisos: first, you may want to limit the total quantity of items as something will happen occasionally that means you need to take action earlier than you thought, and you will need to retrieve an item from the file and action it ahead of the date you originally set. Second, you may want to link it to a diary note, especially if you have no PA.

MAKE USE OF CHECKLISTS

How many times a week do you have to pause and think about how exactly to complete some routine task? Or you do it wrong or incompletely in respect of some detail? Even if you only have a few tasks to complete, checklists will save time, and save it both by preventing those pauses for thought and, more importantly, removing the necessity to do something again. Consider an example. Many companies have a form that is completed when a sales enquiry is received. Completing such a form does not only create a record and act as a prompt to further action, it can also act as a checklist, for instance reminding you to:

— check the enquirer's job title as well as name;
— ask how they heard of the company or product;
— refer to an account number;
— check that you obtain any additional information such as credit details and as many more items as circumstances demand.

Many such routine tasks are not always predictable; converzation with the customer may take all sorts of routes and it is easy to forget those questions that might be considered optional, or at least of lesser importance. So a checklist helps. This can be either a form designed to act as a checklist as its completion proceeds, or a point of reference, literally just a note of what should be done. Some of these you may want to create for yourself and your department, others take the form of company 'standing instructions' and, despite often being categorized as 'yet another memo', may be well worth keeping. Many exist only on computer screens. You may like to make a mental note to look in particular at things that provide assistance outside your own area of expertise. For instance, if you are a dunce with figures, do not throw out that checklist concerning the procedure to reclaim expenses. It might just help you keep track of how much money you've spent so that you can reclaim it, or at least avoid the wrath of an accountant whose system is being ignored—and save you some time. Remember: this kind of documentation is clearly not only useful to record information, but the items listed also act as a prompt to remind you of necessary action. A plethora of such forms can be purchazed as standard items or designed internally to do just what you want.

DIRECTING THE TECHNIQUES

Everything you do in time management terms is designed to affect efficiency, effectiveness and productivity; to enable you to do more and to do everything better than would otherwise be the case, so as to achieve the results your job demands. But there are advantages to be gained en route to these ends, and these are useful in their own right. Bearing them in mind can help you adopt some of the methodology necessary to an organized way of working and make the whole process easier. Such advantages include:

- Having a clear plan, knowing and having an overview of what must be done—the first step to successfully completing the tasks on your list. Such clarity will make adequate preparation more likely and this can reflect directly on achievement.
- Having a clear link between things to do and overall objectives is a sound recipe to keeping on track.
- Being better organized (e.g., not wasting time looking for things).
- Your memory coping better with what you actually need to remember (the systems take care of some of this for you, and it is not necessary to keep everything in your head).
- Being better able to identify and concentrate on the essentials.
- Wasting less energy on irrelevancies.
- Making better decisions about how things should be done (and better business decisions generally).
- Better coordination of tasks (progressing certain things in parallel saves time).
- Having a greater ability to cope with or remove distractions and interruptions.
- Cultivating the habit of greater self-discipline about time matters, which makes consistency of action progressively easier.

— A greater ability to cope with the unexpected and emergency elements of any job.

Any of these are useful, but some may be more useful to you than others, at least at a particular moment or stage. It may be useful to look for the particular advantage you want, wasting less energy on irrelevancies or, more specifically, attending fewer meetings, for example. Or you may wish to adopt methods that will have precisely the impact you want. This is not to say that all those listed above do not have a good general effect on productivity. They do. But they produce additional, and more personal advantage also. You will achieve more and get greater satisfaction from the results you achieve. In addition, you may have more time to develop what you do and how you do it, and motivate yourself and any staff you may have, all of which can potentially improve things still further. And it may remove some of the things that create the feeling that a job is hard work.

4

DECIDING PRIORITIES

Time management is certainly about using methods that will increase the amount of real effective time available to you, but it is also about ordering the work within that time to produce a focus on the right things. As such, it is about priorities as much as it is about anything else. Long term, however, one of the things that really separates the time-efficient from others is their ability to decide on their priorities easily and accurately. That is not something anyone gets 100 per cent correct, and is perhaps something that only comes with experience, but it is worth working towards.

PARETO'S LAW

Before you can work effectively in deciding priorities, you have to come to grips with their importance. This sounds self-explanatory no doubt, and of course you may say some things are obviously more important than others. But it is very easy to underestimate just how much this concept influences what you need to do, indeed just how much it influences your inherent effectiveness. Pareto's law, named after the Italian economist Vilfredo Pareto, is now universally known as the 80/20 rule. It links cause and effect in a ratio and, although this is not represented absolutely accurately in real life, an approximate 80/20 ratio is found in many business activities, sometimes with considerable precision. This means that, for instance, 20 per cent of a company's customers are likely to produce 80 per cent of its revenue; 20 per cent of factory errors are likely to cause 80 per cent of quality rejects.

And it applies specifically in terms of the issues reviewed here also. 20 per cent of meeting time results in about 80 per cent of decisions made; 20 per cent of items to read that pass across your desk produce 80 per cent of the information you need in your work. And, most important of all, 20 per cent of your work time probably contributes around 80 per cent of what is necessary to success in your job. So, it is enormously important to reflect this in the way you operate so that attention is focused on those key issues that have this dramatic effect.

You may not be able to readily identify exactly which of your tasks have this effect. Some things will be clear, others you may need to think about. Have a look at your job description, at your time log too and make yourself think through and decide just what it is about what you do that has the greatest effect. It may not always be obvious for all sorts of reasons. You may take some key things for granted. For instance, forgetting, once they have become a routine, how important they are. Certainly, you are unlikely to find a direct relationship between such a list of key issues and the things your time log shows you spending the most time upon.

Clear objectives and a clear job specification, together with a clear idea of which tasks influence what results and which are key in 80/20 terms, are the only rational bases for deciding priorities. Give yourself these bases and you will be better equipped to work effectively both in terms of time spent on key issues, and in terms of reducing or eliminating corresponding minor matters.

But it is curiously difficult at one level to decide certain priorities. It may help to think here of four categories:

1. urgent and important;
2. urgent but not important;
3. important but not urgent;
4. neither urgent nor important.

Overall, the key is to think first and make considered decisions before letting particular circumstances push you into doing anything, or trying to do everything, first. Things that need actioning fast you must then either do, or delegate, at once; things that can wait should not just be put to one side, but should be planned or scheduled so that they get the time they deserve and then, in turn, get completed as appropriate. This may seem difficult. It is difficult. But the difficulty is, at least in part, psychological. This is a prime area where resolve is more important than technique, and where there are no magic formulae. Making the right judgements in a considered way must become a habit if you are to remain organized in the face of such pressures.

MAKE THE MISCELLANEOUS A PRIORITY

Nothing is perfect and it is inevitable that as you plan and sort and spend most time on priorities, some of the small miscellaneous tasks mount up. If this is what happens—and for many people it is—then it is no good ignoring it and pretending that it does not occur. Rather you need to recognize the situation and decide on a way of dealing with it.

The best way is simply to programme an occasional blitz on the bits and pieces. So, just occasionally clear a few minutes, or an hour if that is what it takes, and go through any outstanding bits and pieces. Write that name in your address book, answer that memo, phone back those people who you wish to keep in touch with but who have not qualified recently as priorities to contact, fill in that analysis form from accounts and all the other things you know tend to get left out and mount up. Ideally, there should be no bits and pieces. If you operate truly effectively then these sorts of things will not be left out. Pigs might fly. If you are realistic then, like me, you will find this useful. Be sure it does not happen too often, but when it does, you can take some satisfaction from the fact that a session to 'blitz the bits' clears the decks and puts you back on top of things, making you more able to deal with the key tasks without nagging distractions.

SCHEDULE—BACKWARDS

Some tasks are straightforward. They consist essentially of one thing and all that matters is deciding when to complete them and getting them done. But many tasks are made up of a number of stages that may be different things you do yourself or with other people. In addition, some stages may be conducted in different locations and the whole process may take days, weeks or months. All of which makes it important to schedule such multi-stage things in the right way if all priority tasks are to be completed on time. What can happen is that you take on a project and begin by believing it is straightforward. Consider an example: you are to produce some sort of newsletter. It is in four stages:

1. deciding the content;
2. writing it;
3. designing it;
4. printing it.

You complete stage one and stage two, but at this point find it has taken somewhat longer than you thought. You hasten into stage three but halfway through it becomes clear that the complete job will not be finished on time. At that point, it may be possible to speed things up, but other priorities could suffer, or the only way to hit the deadline might then be to use additional help, spend additional money or both. What needs to be done is to approach scheduling from the far end of the cycle:

- Start with the deadline.
- Estimate the time of each stage.
- Make sure that the total job fits into the total time available.
- Allow sufficient time for contingencies. Things cannot always be expected to go exactly according to plan.
- Look at the thing in isolation, see how it will fit in with or affect other current projects and responsibilities.

It may be that you need to adjust the way stages work to fit with other matters that are in progress. For example, perhaps a certain stage can be delegated so that this is ready for you to pick up and take it through to the end. A number of options may be possible early on, whereas once you are part way through, the options decline in number and the likelihood of other things being affected increases. All that is necessary here is that sufficient planning time precedes the project, and that in thinking it through you see the overall picture rather than judging whatever it is as a whole and oversimplifying it by just saying 'No problem'.

BE HONEST ABOUT DEADLINES

The biggest problem about deadlines is their urgency—so many things seem to be wanted yesterday that if you are not careful you spend your life running to keep up. As the Red Queen told Alice: '... here you see it takes all the running you can do to stay in the same place. If you want to get somewhere else, you must run twice as fast as that.'

Deadlines must therefore be realistic, which was the burden of the point made in the previous section. Give yourself sufficient time, build in some contingency plans, and then you can deal with the thing properly and still be able to hit the deadline on time. Fine—or is it? There is another common complication to deadlines: people are dishonest about them. In some ways this is understandable—there may be a great deal hanging on a deadline being hit, and not only in terms of results but also of reputations. So, what happens is that if something must be done by the end of the month, it is requested for the 25th 'to be on the safe side'. But this practice, and the people who do it, become known around an office and so the recipient of the deadline decides that a week later is fine. If several people are involved then the misjudgements can get worse as things are passed on and, overall, the chances of missing the date increase. It is ironic, but what starts out as a genuine attempt to ensure a deadline is met, ends up actually making it less likely that it will be.

The moral is clear. In any group with which you are associated, try to make sure the situation about deadlines is clear and open, and that everyone approaches the situation similarly. If something needs completing on the 10th of the month, say so. This not only makes it more certain that the deadline involved will be hit, in part because people like this approach and commit to it more certainly, but also prevents other things being at risk because time is being spent chasing a deadline that is not, in fact, the real one. There is sufficient pressure in most offices without compounding the problem artificially. While many, many things have to be completed by a deadline, there are some where exactly how they are done affects how long they take. And there may be more of these than you think. However, consider first those things that must be done but might be done differently from the way they are undertaken today.

REVIEW TASK METHODOLOGY

Consider the example of my writing work again. Obviously, the changes that might be made to any task will depend on the nature of it, but all sorts of things can be worthwhile, for example:

- Systematizing a task that was previously more random or circuitous.
- Changing actual methods.
- Working with someone else.
- Lower standards. One method may achieve perfection, another—faster—one may achieve a lesser, but perfectly acceptable, result and sometimes save money.
- Subcontract. In other words pay an external supplier to do something that they can do quicker, and sometimes cheaper and better, than you.

Again, such a list could go on and you may be able to think of routes to action that suit your particular job and work best for you. However, the principle of checking to see if there is a better way of doing something is sound. Maybe if you select certain tasks and swap them with a colleague this will bring a fresh mind to bear and prompt new thinking about methodology; you do something for them and they for you. However it happens, make it happen, for there is never only one right way of doing anything for ever, and improved methodology can be a great time saver.

ELIMINATE THE UNNECESSARY

Most people will deny, if asked, that they spend time doing things that are unnecessary; after all it seems absurd. But it does happen. And it happens for all sorts of reasons. Consider a few examples:

- *Habit.* You have always attended a monthly meeting, read a regularly circulated report, checked certain information, filed certain items and kept in touch with certain people. And it is easy for things to run on, repeating automatically without thought and for such things to take up time unnecessarily.
- *Insurance.* You do things for protective reasons. In case something goes wrong, in case someone asks why, in case... what? Sometimes the reason is not clear, there is just a feeling that it is safer to do something than not. Filing and documenting things are examples of this.
- *Avoidance.* The real reason for something to be done has long disappeared, but continuing to do it means you have no time—and excuse—to take on or try out something new and perhaps risky. Be honest, have you really never put of doing something new?
- *Expectation.* You do things not because of their real worth, but because it is, or you feel it is, expected of you. In a team environment you do not want to let others down, though you will let things down more by ignoring priorities.
- *Appearances.* You do things because they are 'good things' to be involved with, perhaps politically, and every organization has some politics. Your position and people's perception of you around the organization are important, but you must not overdo this kind of involvement, not least because

it can become self-defeating, being seen as the ego trip of someone who has nothing better to do.

All of these and more may occur and, make no mistake, there are no doubt valid reasons under each heading—you really do need to attend some meetings simply to demonstrate commitment and this is a tangible and priority result. But... but, this is an area you need to be quite tough about. Are there any things you are doing that you can stop doing without affecting the results significantly? For most people an honest appraisal shows the answer to be 'yes', so review it immediately if you have not done so for a while, and regularly afterwards to ensure that unnecessary tasks are not creeping in again.

How is this done? Very simply, you ask why? Why is something being done? And if the answer is because that is the way it is, that is the system, or, worst of all, that is the way it has always been done, then ask again. If you cannot really find a better reason then the task may well be a candidate for elimination. Failing that, maybe you can do it less often, in less detail or otherwise adjust the approach to save time and allow attention to be given to the priorities. This is another area that can start from the time log; it is not just what you are doing that matters, but the time it takes. If you are ruthless about this kind of questioning and honest about the answers then time may be saved in this way.

KEEP DISTANCE

One particular kind of task may very sensibly be categorized as unnecessary, at least to you. Black holes, collapsed stars so massive and with such powerful gravity that they pull in everything and even light cannot escape from them, make the old expression about going down the plug hole seem pretty small beer. In most offices, there are corporate equivalents of this phenomenon, 'black hole jobs' that suck in all the time you can think of and more. Watch out for them and beware—just like real black holes, if you get too near there is no going back and an involvement means all your other plans have to be put on hold. What kind of jobs warrant this description? They include projects that:

- involve a number of different, and complex, tasks;
- may be contentious;
- are impossible to complete and please everyone;
- may be ruinous of reputations;
- take up a quite disproportionate amount of time.

They encompass a range of things from organizing the company's twentieth-anniversary celebrations to moving the company to new offices. Such things have to be done, but they often call for 'volunteers'. This can mean the Managing Director suggests it, in public, in a way that makes refusal risky: 'It is only a suggestion, of course, but do bear in mind who's making it.' At this point, others heave sighs of relief and resolve not to get involved even in a tiny support role. You will know, if you have any wits at all, the kind of tasks in your office that have these characteristics and you should, if you value your ability to keep on top of your other tasks, plan to be well away whenever there is a danger of you getting lumbered with one. Do not say you have not been warned.

BE CONFIDENT

The best time managers organize successfully to concentrate time and energy on their priorities and one reason they do so seems to be an ability to make prompt and firm decisions about what should be priorities. Others use up hours of valuable time not only deciding what should come first, but reviewing the decision again and again to double-check it. Of course, circumstances change and some ongoing review may be necessary but it does not help, as the saying has it, to keep digging up the plant to look at the roots to check if it is growing well. The decision process starts with review and analysis. Remembering that you can only do one thing at a time, you must be clear what the key factors on your list are and which are in fact most important, and constitute the real priorities. Having considered all sides of this thoroughly, you need to make a decision. There is no reason at that point to doubt that it is other than a good one.

So, make the decision, stick to it, and get on with the task. The quicker you do that the sooner you will be able to move on down the list. Much is written about stress in the workplace. Stress is a reaction to circumstances rather than the circumstances themselves. You should be able to say that you:

- know your priorities;
- have made work planning decisions sensibly, based on reasonable and thorough consideration of all the facts;
- are sure there is no more, for the moment, you can do to make things easier;
- know that as you proceed with the task you are going to do it effectively and that the methodology you will use makes sense.

This should then allow you to be comfortable about the process, and to reject any tendency to stress. Trying to work at something while worried that there may be greater priorities, knowing that a variety of other things are queuing up for attention but are as yet unsorted, and having any doubts about the way you are doing things is a sure recipe for stress. Keep calm by keeping organized and you will be better placed to maintain and increase your effectiveness.

❖❖❖

5

MINIMIZE PAPERWORKS

Letters, memos, faxes, reports, forms, proposals, and more, all combine to create a steady stream of paperwork across your desk. If you are not reading things, you are writing them, and if you are not doing that you are processing things that involve paperwork. All this can take up a significant proportion of your working day. In time management terms the job is to minimize it.

Perhaps the first thing to ask in this area is simply: is all your paperwork really necessary? Let it be clear straight away, much of it will be. But some paperwork can be eliminated, and often all that is necessary is to pause for a second before you write something, and ask yourself whether what you are about to do is really necessary. Have a look at what is on your desk, see how much of it is not really necessary, think how much of it could achieve its aims in some other way. Yet, someone is sending all this to your desk and is presumably well intentioned in doing so.

So, what do you do about it? The key alternative to written communication is the telephone; it is usually much quicker to lift the telephone than to write something, and, as not everything needs a written record, this is one of the surest ways of reducing paperwork. It is also worth a note here about the now ubiquitous e-mail.

It seems that an altogether less formal style has developed for e-mail, one that is perfectly acceptable internally in a big company with a number of offices, and between external organizations, as a quick form of communication where brevity is essential. Brevity saves time, but it must be easily understood too. Print out and file e-mails where appropriate, and keep those listed in your computer manageable.

Two other points are worth a mention. In the interests of slowing the destruction of forests to make paper, as much as time, consider copies. It is one thing to write to someone, but it is the circulation of copies that feeds the proliferation of paperwork as much as anything. Think before you list half the company; who really needs a copy?

BE BRAVE

Your written communication will be less time-consuming if it is not only brief but, choosing my words carefully, succinct and precise and, of course, clear (this is not the place for a treatise on making communications understandable, but communication should never be assumed to be easy. It is often the reverse, and misunderstandings must be responsible for a massive amount of wasted time as things are queried and clarified). This is worth a short (sic) paragraph here.

An example makes the point: Jasmin writes to Chandran prior to a meeting asking when his flight arrives and whether he would like to be met at the airport. So often the reply will be along the lines of:

> Dear Mr Chandran,
>
> Thank you for your kind letter of 24 April 2011 about my forthcoming visit to your offices next week on Thursday 30 April. I am pleased to say that all my

> travel arrangements are now complete – you may remember I was having trouble with one of the connections – and I now have full details. I arrive on Flight 915 at 10.00 am. This should suit our lunch meeting well and not make any problem with the timing. With regard to your kind offer to meet me, perhaps I could say how grateful I would be for your assistance in this regard...

And so on. If the two know each other even a little, surely there can be nothing wrong with something that says:

> Dear Mr Chandran,
>
> It was good to hear from you. I arrive on Flight 915 at 10.00 am on 30 April. It would be a great help to be met at the airport; I will look out for your driver. Many thanks, I look forward to seeing you soon...

In the second example, the information is clear and consise. It saves time, and may well be one-third or one-quarter of the length of the first one. And it took less time to write and send.

MINIMAL MEMOS

The memo makes up a major part of the paperwork in many offices. Here is a simple idea that can save even more time. Assume you receive a memo – a full page of some colleague's meanderings no doubt – and what it says is just: 'Can you attend a meeting of the planning committee at 3pm this coming Friday?' Assume that you can and are prepared to attend. Now all you need to do is photocopy the memo that came to you, write 'TO:' at the top and ring the name of the original sender, write 'FINE, SEE YOU THERE' at the bottom and sign it. If you really want to be rash with time, take an extra second and add a ring round your message to highlight it. Then send it back.

We often see people laboriously preparing typed and sometimes over-long memos when this kind of procedure will do very well; some companies have pre-printed sheets for their memos that are designed to take a reply. E-mail is helping this process; many e-mails are brief, and this developing style seems set to become a habit. Remember, however, the comments about the time-wasting tendencies of e-mail already made. In such circumstances you can always telephone, though consider who it is, how long they will chat and whether they would appreciate confirmation in writing for the record.

MINIMIZE PAPER HANDLING

Here is an interesting experiment you can try. Select 10 or so items that come across your desk today, a mixture of letters, memos and documents, all of which demand some action on your part, and mark them all with a red spot in the top right-hand corner. Then simply deal with them as normal. And every time you touch them thereafter add another red spot to the top right-hand corner. As time passes you will then produce a count of how many times things go through your hands. For example, a letter arrives today and:

- you read it;
- you decide not to deal with it immediately but put it with a job on which you intend to spend time in the afternoon;
- in the afternoon you make a start, work out what needs to be done but are interrupted;
- the letter joins a number of items that overrun the day and you pick it up again the following morning, and so it goes on.

In this case we are imagining just a simple letter. In other cases, projects and processes span weeks or months; you can imagine the incidence of red spots. This is known as the 'measles test' and it can help you identify how your way of handling things affects the time that dealing with them takes. Sometimes the multiple 'spotting' is necessary, but other cases may well surprise you because you had no idea just how often some things cross your desk before they are resolved. The first step towards change is to know where change should be applied. The information gained in this way will be useful. Sometimes improvement is easy, for example the use of a Prompt File will cure some 'spotting'. If you have a clear plan and a system for categorizing your work then things should be dealt with immediately, or held for some reason and then dealt with. If this is applied rigorously, then the time taken up by papers being handled many times will be reduced. For a lot of people there are a great many links between different items and areas; indeed an element of some jobs involves creatively seeing links that can be turned into opportunities, and with the process of what is called synergy.

All of this may demand sufficient review of the situations represented by your paperwork for this opportunity process to be possible. So this rule, like some others, must not be applied slavishly. You need sufficient sight of some items to operate effectively and must be careful not to reduce paper handling in a way you feel does not suit or work well in your individual job.

REDUCE FILE WORKS

A frightening statistic emerging from a survey in one multinational giant showed that only 10 per cent of the papers put into filing were ever referred to again; this in an organization proud of its efficiency—what hope for ordinary mortals? This means that 90 per cent could have been destroyed, and the cost of 'keeping them at the right temperature in comfortable surroundings', as the survey called it, is enormous.

By all means let a secretary design or help with the design of a system, but to achieve consistency you should always decide what goes where. Do the papers about that reorganization go under R for reorganization, O for organization or office, E for efficiency drive, or B for boss's pet projects? There are often serious problems here, as anyone who has tried to locate a file, say, a year old, knows; few have memories that will hold this kind of detail forever. So, get the system right. It is difficult to generalise, you may need account flies, project flies or a dozen more; or all of these. It is usually better to have a number of categories, each A-Z, rather than one giant system that has to cope with everything. As you review potential filing material you only really have three options for action:

- do not file it, throw it away;
- file it with no thought for how long it will stay there;
- file it with a clear indication of a destroy date.

Consider what is on or around your desk at present. How much of it could you throw away right now? Probably the answer is very little. But imagine those same papers in the future, how many of them will you need in six months, in a year, in two years? Here the honest answer will be fewer and getting even fewer as you go into the future. So why not throw more away?

Think about where else things are held. If you need to check something in, say, a regular financial summary only once in three months, why even have a file on it if you know you can get it from the accountant in 30 seconds? Think about the things you hold 'just in case'. In your heart you probably know you are not at all bad at judging what will be required, yet you still keep too much. Trust your instincts, remember the old saying: if it looks like a duck and quacks, then it probably is a duck. If you are 99 per cent sure it is going to be rubbish very soon, you are probably right; after all, they are your papers. So throw them away.

But if you are wrong and need something you have thrown away, which may do more than waste time, consider some insurance. There are two systems that will provide this. First, batch filing—this is where filing is not done too early. Everything is put in simple A–Z order in a batch file and only filed after, say, a month (you pick the time). But before it is filed you look through it to see what you still want to keep. After even one month, you might be surprized how much you ditch. This is kept for a fixed length of time, maybe a year in quarterly flies to make it more manageable. Every time the fourth quarter file is full, the first quarter file is thrown away and you start a new quarter file with the current material. Either system or both may suit you. Many systems benefit from a destroy system. This can be done by setting dates (perhaps in year batches) or even very simply by capacity. The drawer is always just on full, and this corresponds well with how long the contents appear to remain useful and no one has to waste any time over it.

This area must be systemized on a basis that works for your office. If things are well ordered, if you can find what you want and do not have to spend time constantly resorting the system to make room for more and more, then it will work well and you will run it and it will not run you. Order in the filing must save time. Note: if your flies are, even in part, in your computer, consider what printed versions you should have—and take regular back-up flies and store them separately.

KEEP PAPERS TIDY

It is a small point perhaps, but you can waste some time

hunting for papers and re-collating papers that have got out of order in this sort of way. But papers must be kept tidy. Do not keep too much together, and worry in particular about flies and papers that travel about with you both around and out of the office. The more things you have to work on in parallel, the more your current papers need organizing neatly. If you only get one file out at a time and work on that until it is neatly replaced by something else, then it is less of a problem. If you are paid to keep many balls in the air at once, then it is vital. Time management is, in this respect, similar to juggling. If there are a lot of balls in the air and one is dropped, more tend to follow. The more you have on the go, the greater the disruption and waste of time if something becomes disorganized. Keep papers physically under control.

COMPUTERISE OFFICE WORKS

It became one of the great 20th century myths that computers would transform office work, and make everything fast and efficient to action. But like other great promises it is not entirely to be trusted. Now, I have nothing against computers and there are things that one cannot now imagine working any other way, and yet... there are questions, certainly as far as efficiency and time utilization are concerned, at desk level for the individual executive. There are examples of things now available that manifestly work well:

- computerized databases that can be accessed on a desktop PC and dramatically reduce the time needed to sort through, analyse or communicate with those names on them;
- graphics programs that can turn a set of conflusing figures into a graph and impart a key point in a moment;

- desktop publishing (DTP), which means documentation can be produced in-house at the touch of a button, removing the need to liaise with three separate outside suppliers;
- e-mail systems, which can allow easy, rapid communication with a branch office, say, or overseas contact, and allow you to peep into their flies;
- computerized versions of things like drawing diagrams, analyzing figures, interpreting statistics (and playing noughts and crosses!), which make their manual equivalents look positively quaint.

You can probably think of many more. Some you will use and regard as routine, and many can save time. Yet, there are systems that for all their cleverness do not fit their role so well. Think of some of the systems you may be frustrated by as a customer, in the bank, insurance company or hotel. Consider a hotel account. They are, presumably, efficient for the hotel but many are very difficult to fathom without a degree in abbreviations. Customer service suffers. So there is another side to computers; you need expert help to set up many systems, there is a high capital cost though this is coming down, and they are all too readily used as an excuse for not doing things. Above all, they take time to set up and the equation of time must be carefully balanced to see what makes best sense.

There are things in this area that are great time savers. There are also pitfalls, costly in time, for the unwary. By all means use what you can, check out new things as they become available, but consider the alternatives as well and you may conclude some of them still hold good. If you can find that telephone number faster just by turning it up in a pocket notebook, why not do just that until something comes along that really is better for you?

DO NOT DUPLICATE INFORMATION

There is time expended in maintaining any information system. If the information is being recorded in identical or similar form in several different places, then the time is longer. This is worth checking, and there is a quick check you can run in a few moments. Rule up a matrix with information on one axis and places where it is kept on the other. If this produces columns of ticked boxes, then you may be holding information in too many places.

Such an analysis will quickly show the extent of any kind of duplication—and the sheer extent of the recording going on. If you then think about where information is most often sought, you may well find that only a minority of places originally listed are highlighted. This in turn poses questions about the other places where the information appears. How many of them can be scrapped or reduced? Time and neglect, or if you want to feel better about it, concentration on other matters, allow a proliferation of systems and information over time, sometimes far beyond what is really useful at present. Incidentally, another area to watch is computer information systems in which the technical ability to include extra information is often sufficient reason for it to be included. It is the use that is made of such sources that is important.

DO NOT PROLIFERATE INFORMATION

Sometimes tasks seem important and then something happens that shows that this was not true at all, or perhaps not true any more. One thing that sometimes happens is that time is wasted because once something is originated then thinking about it ceases. The Managing Director denied all knowledge of this, but his secretary, overhearing the request, said she held a file of the information. We checked and there it was. It arrived on her desk each month and she filed it. He had looked at it and put it in his secretary's filing tray, and she had opened a file for it. The sales office produced it again the next month, sent it to the MD's office, but his secretary filed it without showing it to him. This had then been repeated every month for two years! It took someone in the sales office several hours each month to complete the work to produce the figures, and, after the first time, it had all been a complete waste.

Such situations continue all too easily once the initial moment has passed just who was at fault? The sales office, the MD, the secretary? All three? It just *happened* they might say, but, more to the point, could it have been prevented? You should make a rule that whenever you are asked or need to provide any information to anyone, you make a diary note to check at some time in the future—in 6 or 12 months perhaps—whether it is still necessary. Find out whether it still needs to be sent:

— with the same frequency;

— to all the listed people;

— in as much detail.

Any change that will save time is worthwhile and you may find that it is simply not necessary any more. Very few people will ask for information to stop coming to them, but if asked may well admit that they can happily do without it. Be aware of this sort of thing, or it is quite possible that all around your organization things will be repeated unnecessarily.

DO NOT PUT IT IN WRITING

While he had lavished care and attention on the report, he was unprepared for this and his spur of the moment presentation was not as fluent as he would have wished, the matter to which the report referred was dropped and the report was never read. He was naturally aggrieved and resented the incident—with some cause perhaps.

Certainly, management ought to consider the time-wasting consequences of its action, decisions and requests. What avoids something taking up time for you may land someone else with a great deal of extra work. If you are a manager, your responsibility for good time utilization covers the team. It is little good being productive yourself if everyone else is tied up with all sorts of unnecessary tasks and paperwork jobs need to be done, action taken, consideration given and in many cases written instructions, guidelines or confirmation are not simply necessary, they are vital. But on other occasions that may well not be the case. This kind of thing can often happen. Time may be wasted unless the instigator of such action thinks first and only specifies written details of something if it is really necessary. Similarly, those in receipt of such requests should not be afraid to ask, and check whether such exercises are really necessary. Whichever category you are in, and it may well be both, give it a thought. Of course, there are other considerations.

USE WASTE-PAPER BASKET

The waste-paper basket. It helps efficiency and time if your desk and office are tidy, if what you need is neatly and accessibly placed—a place for everything and everything in its place—but not if such good order is submerged under sheer quantity of paper, most of it of a 'just in case' nature.

All sorts of things cross your desk: magazines, direct mail, items marked 'To read and circulate' and 'For information', copies of things that are of no real relevance to you and minutes of meetings that you wish had never taken place. Much of this causes you to pause for far too long, creating heaps and extra filing trays and bundles in your briefcase. It is better to deal with things early rather than later. When it has mounted up it is always going to be more difficult to get through, and an immediate decision will keep the volume down, for example:

- If you are on a circulation list and do not want to look at something today, then add your name further down the list and pass it on; it will get back to you later when you may be less busy.
- At least check a magazine once, maybe you can tear out an article or two and throw the rest away.
- Consider very carefully whether the vast plethora of things that 'might be useful' are, in fact, ever likely to be; either file them or throw them away.

All these kinds of thinking and action help, but most people are conservative and reluctant to throw things away. Unless you are very untypical, there will be things on and around your desk right now that could be thrown out. Have a look, and, as you look, do some throwing. Make a full WPB a target for the end of the day. Imagine it has a scale running down the inside to show how full it is. This scale could almost be graduated, not in volume, but in minutes saved. The paperless office may still be a way of; in the meantime, keeping what there is under control is certainly an important part of the time management process.

6

TIME MANAGEMENT FOR STAFF

Every organization works on deadlines. An individual constantly needs to be on his toes to finish off assignments within stipulated time frame. It is essential for employees to understand the value of time for them to do well and make a mark of their own at the workplace.

In an organization you will encounter people of all sorts Some you will get on with, some you will not; some will help you, inform you, or teach you; some will infuriate you; some you will work with, getting things done that would not happen otherwise. But, male or female, young or old, senior or junior—all will waste your time. Some will do so intentionally, others unwittingly, but it will happen. Because people interactions in business are vital, there is no way of avoiding them, but you have to work with people in a way that anticipates and minimizes the disruptive effect they can have on your time. Some will be most appropriate if you manage other people, others are more generally applicable; all will save you time.

An organization is a club. Colleagues are acquaintances or friends and work can be fun, and this makes for problems as, for example, 'Good morning' turns into half the morning disappearing in chatter. It is an area where a time log may provide surprising information. On the other hand, you do need to keep things in proportion, curtail excesses and beware those moments when the danger is greatest—time will be really wasted. These include:

- first thing in the morning, when greetings tend to turn into an in-depth analysis of the meal, date, TV or movie, sporting event or disaster of the previous evening;
- breaks, when the coffee comes round or people gather around the drinks machine;
- lunch, when even the process of discussing when to go, with whom, and where, assumes time-consuming proportions;
- the end of the day when everyone is getting tired and a chat is a welcome excuse to wind down early.

There are places too where you are prone to get caught and converzation runs on. In some companies, Reception acts as a sort of plaza with people coming and going through it in different directions using their meeting as an excuse for a chat.

Because people's work patterns are different, moments when you have time for a chat may not suit others and vice versa. There needs to be mutual respect for people's time and concentration around an office, and everyone can play a part in fostering such a culture. Not only does this waste their time, but what you intended to be a two-minute pause may very easily turn into half an hour, two cups of coffee and, even if some of the converzation is useful, a major disruption of two people's schedules. So beware and be careful—there is no need to be stand-offish or to screen out useful converzations, but remember that this is a major factor eating away at productivity, and act accordingly.

INFORMAL CONTACT

You do need to see and talk to people. But, like so much else, how and when this is organized should be a conscious plan, one conditioned not least by the time that will be taken up. How do you approach this? This has become a technique in its own right, with its own abbreviation: MBWA. These initials stand for 'management by walking about', and it describes the need for management, perhaps especially senior management, to keep in touch at a direct and personal level with the other departments and people with whom they work. However good the management control systems in an organization, there is no substitute for going and seeing and hearing for yourself what is going on, and what problems and opportunities exist.

Management can very often become protected and cloistered to the point that they have no genuine feel for how other parts of the organization work. So not only is this sound advice, but it is a real aid to communication, and it can save time. Being in touch makes a real difference to your ability to operate, so the balance of time here—taken and saved—is likely to be productive. This is especially true if you can find ways of creating opportunities for this that serve more than one purpose. At the end of the second day, drinks were available and at one moment as everyone was chatting, the Managing Director interrupted his discussion with one of his people to make notes—they had stumbled on a useful point and he noted it for later follow-up. This happened quite naturally as the chat mixed with more serious comment.

The point here was that the Managing Director, doubtless a busy man, consciously saw such a gathering as serving a double purpose: he was happy to support training, but more ready to do so if it provided an opportunity for some of the 'walking about' he felt was necessary anyway. He might have considered that giving just an introduction was not time well spent, but the addition of drinks and discussion—in fact taking longer—made it serve two purposes and become well worthwhile.

MAKING A WORKING LUNCH WORK

An army marches on its stomach. In business too, we all have to pause now and then to refuel. What has this to do with time management? Consider the following phrases. First, First, 'business lunch'. For most people this conjures up something expensive, lengthy, and substantial. If you add in the time taken to get to such an event, then the total time involved is something to be considered very carefully. You need to think about whether to accept such invitations, or how often to do so. You may need to meet with the person concerned, but there may be other ways to achieve this. And you certainly need to think twice before you issue such invitations yourself. Again, the first question is whether a meeting is necessary, then whether it needs to be at lunch. Entertaining is, without a doubt, important. Some contacts (customers, suppliers and others) will not rate the business relationship so highly if you appear to take it for granted. Yet time is finite and you cannot do this every time you think of it. Each occasion should result from a considered decision and be worthwhile in its own right. Also consider simpler options. A meal out in a good restaurant or hotel may be too time-consuming for your contact. What simpler options are there? Something in the office perhaps? It must be done well, but it does not need to be a gigantic meal or a time-consuming occasion to meet its objectives. You may well find this option is welcomed by some of your contacts.

Second, 'working lunch'. This is more often internal, and can be very simple—an urgent meeting scheduled for an appropriate hour with just coffee and sandwiches provided makes for productivity. Similarly, you may opt to go out for a simple snack with a colleague and do so to discuss a particular matter, often one that has previously escaped fitting into your schedule. All this is useful. Sometimes lunchtime needs to be something of a pause, but remember with around 220 working days in the year, an hour for lunch on each would add up to more than 25 working days! So, it is certainly an area to think about extremely carefully. A final, cautionary, note: watch what you drink at lunchtime. Alcohol may help relaxation but falling asleep at your desk later will certainly not improve productivity!

CONSIDER A DAY OUT

Entertaining was just referred to, but it can take many forms and some of them are a good deal more time-consuming than lunch. Corporate entertaining can include a wide variety of things from a night at the opera, to an evening in a karaoke bar; from a day at the races to a golf afternoon. Because they involve a very real cost, such things certainly need thinking about, but so too do the time considerations.

Take a golf outing as an example. Much business may really be conducted on the golf course, and I am not suggesting that such activity is never useful and should be entirely rejected, but its real merits do need assessing. It is not enough that you or your contact will enjoy whatever it is. Ask:

- What will come of it?
- Will it genuinely move the relationship forward?
- Is there another way of achieving the same effect with less time expenditure?
- Can anyone else do it?

NO CONFLICT

Now listen, pay attention. It is no good just sitting there lazily scanning the pages, you have to read this properly and... Not a good start. Sometimes an approach that is designed to get straight to the point and therefore not waste time has the reverse effect. It rubs people up the wrong way, and can produce misunderstanding, dissent or argument that in turn take time to resolve and the original intention goes out the window. Conflict is not, in fact, entirely bad. It can act as a catalyst to debate, it can help promote creativity and prompt a drive for the results necessary in business. But there is a real difference between this and allowing unnecessary conflict to disrupt the smooth running of things and your time being affected along with it. I am not suggesting here that the wrong decisions should be made for the sake of a quiet life, but in a number of areas conflict is to be avoided, for example:

- In communications. It may be necessary to persuade rather than cajole, and time taken to do so successfully may pay dividends.
- Office politics can become intrusive and time-consuming; though ignoring it is dangerous in other ways, it must be kept in its place.
- Personalities can become more important than issues; commercial reason must dictate most of what directs an organization, and untangling personality factors once they have got out of hand takes time.
- Sectional interests also have to be watched.

Take this last as a simple example. Imagine that some internal reorganization is to change the physical layout of an office—departments are going to move and, not surprisingly, sections are worried about the priority they will be given and the new conditions they will find. Yet, there are entirely practical issues too. The design department needs good lighting, the customer services department needs the most telephones, a department with large amounts of stock in and out may need to be on the ground floor, to take some very general ones. If consideration of what will be decided, any discussions, meetings and everything to do with the process, can be kept primarily on a practical basis (there are other issues, of course); if conflict, in this case about personal issues, can be avoided, the time taken to sort the whole thing out will almost certainly be less. This has wide implications, but shows the merit of always bearing in mind the time element of everything you touch. Circumstances that can create time-wasting because of conflict can be momentary, something only demanding a moment's thought to avoid, or more intractable, demanding real effort and willpower to avoid when you are itching to draw up battle lines. In either case, you should be on the lookout for such circumstances and act to avoid their worst effects. Next, a number of points are investigated predominantly for those who, as managers, have other people reporting to them. Many of the points made will have relevance to others on the receiving end of such a relationship, or whose job is likely to include such responsibilities at some time in the future.

SELECT THE RIGHT PEOPLE

The logical starting point is perhaps when such relationships are created. Finding the right person for any job is a vital and complex business, one too often underestimated. It means:

- performance being adversely affected;
- time taken up trying to correct the situation, and ultimately in discipline proceedings;

- replacing an inappropriate staff member;
- plugging gaps while all this is going on.

Recruiting and selecting takes time, but it is time well spent. Maybe, also, you want to select people who are themselves good at managing time. This can certainly enhance the strength of any team you manage. Anyway, leaving the details of recruitment and selection aside, with the people in place you can consider what aspects of management are linked most closely to time management. One such is a key aspect of communication.

GIVE CLEAR INSTRUCTIONS

There is an old saying that there is never time to do anything properly, but there must always be time to do it again. Nothing is more likely to end up being redone than not making it clear to people what they had to do in the first place. It has already been said here that communication is not easy, but the responsibility for getting it right is with the communicator—and that, if you are issuing instructions, is you. Similarly, if people do not really understand and fail to query it, perhaps because they are worried you will blame them, then that is also your fault because you should make it clear that in such circumstances it is the way they should proceed. So, instructions should be clear and people should be told:

- what needs to be done;
- why it needs to be done;
- how it should be done;
- when it should be completed.

Before leaving the point, ask if it is clear—get some feedback. Any short-cut of this sequence must be based on genuine knowledge or familiarity, not simply an assumption that all will be well. Good clear instructions save time; written guidelines do the same and for some jobs they are useful. This last is especially true of awkward or difficult jobs that are performed regularly but not often. It is not that complicated, but frankly it is difficult to do after the time gap usually involved without reference to a chart of diagrams that came with the machine and that shows clearly the sequence of actions needed to complete the task. The moment taken to get this chart out is tiny, much less than even minor pause for puzzlement about how to make the change without it, and it is all too easy with such a task to get in a real muddle and waste a considerable amount of time. Moral: all instructions, in whatever form, must be clear.

MAKING DELEGATION SUCCESSFUL

If a task simply has to be done, but you cannot get to it, then the best way to give yourself more time is to delegate it to someone else. This is eminently desirable and yet, for some, curiously difficult. What are the pros and cons?

First, the advantages. Consider these by asking yourself what sort of manager you want to work for yourself. You could probably list a great many qualities: someone who is fair, who listens, who is decisive, good at their job and so on—but I bet you would put someone who delegates high on the list. The opposite is a boss who hangs on to everything, does not involve you, is probably secretive and generally not the sort of person you would want to work for at all. So, if you delegate effectively, there are major advantages in other ways: motivation and the chance to tackle new things for one, as well as the time you will save.

Second, the difficulties. Delegating is a risk. Something may go wrong and what is more, as the manager, you may be blamed. So, despite the fact that going about it the right way will minimize the risk, there is temptation to hang on to things. This makes for problems in two ways. You have too much to do, and particularly too much at the more routine end, keeping you from giving things that are clear priorities the attention you know they deserve. And staff do not like it, so motivation—and productivity on the things they are doing—will also be adversely affected.

But there is another important and significant reason why delegation sometimes does not happen. This is fear—not that the other person will not be able to cope, but that they will cope too well, that they will improve the method, that they will do things more quickly, more thoroughly and better in some way than you. If you are honest, you may admit this is a real fear too. Certainly, it is a common one. Though it is precisely how innovation can occur. It is not a reason that should put you of delegating—the potential rewards are too great. The amount you can do if you delegate successfully is way beyond the improvement in productivity you can hope to achieve in any other way. So, it is a vital area. But what about something delegated that does go better? So much to the good, this is one of the key ways that progress is made in organizations as new people, new ways and new thinking are brought to bear on tasks. Without it, organizations would become stultified and unable to cope with change. And besides, as a manager you should be the reason they are able to make this happen. It is your selection, development, counselling and management that create and maintain a strong and effective team; and this is something for which you deserve credit.

Making delegation successful needs a considered and systematic approach to the process. What does successful delegation achieve? There are several key results. Delegation:

- creates, for those to whom matters are delegated, opportunity for development;

- — builds morale through the motivational effect of greater job satisfaction, and achievement long and short term in the job;
- — has broader motivational effects around a team, as well as on the individual;
- — for the delegator, concentrates time and effort on those aspects of their job that are key to the achievement of objectives;
- — brings a more considered, or creative, approach to bear, uncluttered by matters that may distract or prevent a broad brush or longer-term perspective.

You can probably think of specific advantages springing from these kinds of general effects in your own job. If the time gains to be made from delegation seem inadequate to make you do it, or do it as much as you should, maybe this will produce additional pause for thought. Despite the several and considerable advantages delegation can bring, it is not without its risks. This element of risk makes it difficult to accomplish, but several factors can help:

1. *Minimizing the risks.* There is always the possibility that delegation will not work. After all, it passes on 'the right to be wrong' as it were, by putting someone else in the driving seat. So, if a misjudgement is made about the choice of what is to be delegated, to whom it is to be delegated or how the process will be carried out, things may end up with mistakes being made, and time being wasted as a result. The net intention from all this must be to minimize the inherent risks, first by selecting tasks that are suitable for delegation. In most jobs there will be certain things that should sensibly be omitted. These include:

   - — matters key to overall results generation or control;

- staff discipline matters;
- certain contentious issues (e.g. staff grievances);
- confidential matters.

Then, in picking the best person to whom to delegate, you should ask questions such as:

- Have they undertaken similar tasks in the past?
- Do they have the necessary knowledge, experience and capability?
- Is it too much to cope with at once?
- Is prior training (however informal) necessary?
- Do they want to do more? (Or should they?)
- Will they be acceptable to others involved and will it be accepted also as a fair opportunity amongst peers?

Thereafter, perhaps the greatest guarantee of success is clear communication, and that means more widely than just with the person involved. Others may have to know what is going on and have to trust in the person's ability to do something. Messages may need to be passed up and down and across the line to ensure total clarity. Make sure there is nothing left out regarding authority, responsibility and that, above all, the individual concerned knows why the job is necessary and why they are doing it. And, as the result of any briefing, be confident that they are able to do it satisfactorily.

Any explanation needs to make clear whether what is being done is a one-of exercise, perhaps in an emergency, or ultimately a permanent addition to the existing set of responsibilities. Remember, delegation is more than simple work allocation and, as such, can have implications for such matters as job descriptions, salary and employment conditions. Assuming that delegation is well chosen and communicated, the next step is to keep in touch, at least initially, with how things are going.

2. *Monitoring progress.* Once something has been passed over, keeping in touch can easily be forgotten, and when done it can present certain problems. It must be done, in a word, carefully. If it is not, then it will smack of interference and may doom the whole process. The simplest way to monitor in an acceptable way is to build in any necessary checks at the time of the original briefing and handover. From the beginning, ask for interim reports at logical points. Do not simply arrive unannounced at someone's desk and ask to see the file. Let them bring things to you, at prearranged moments. If they have been well briefed, know what is expected and to what standards, then they can deliver in a way that either duplicates past practice, or brings something new to the activity. Either may be appropriate in the short term, though, as nothing lasts for ever, new thinking is usually to be encouraged once the person has a real handle on the basics.

It may be necessary to let things proceed, to bite your tongue and resist taking the whole matter back during this stage as you see things proceeding in a way that may well differ, if only a little, from the way in which you would have done the job. The ultimate results make all this worthwhile, and not just in time terms but in terms of growth and development within the workplace. So far so good. If all goes well surely there is nothing more to be done? Wrong. The process must be evaluated.

3. *Evaluating how delegation has worked.* Once sufficient time has gone by and you can assess how things have gone, a number of questions should be asked. These can usefully include:
   - Has the task been completed satisfactorily?
   - Did it take an acceptable amount of time?
   - Does it indicate the person concerned could do more?
   - Are there other tasks that could be delegated along the same route?
   - What has been the effect on others (e.g. are others wanting more responsibility)?
   - Is there any documentation change necessary as a result?
   - Has any new or revised methodology been created and are there implications arising from this (e.g. a change to standing instructions)?
   - Overall, what has the effect been on productivity? In other words: what have you done with the time saved? There is little to be gained by delegating if you only end up submerged in more detail and having little or nothing of real substance to show for the change.

Similarly, should the process not be a success, questions should be asked about what went wrong and they too need to address both sides, asking not just what did someone do wrong or misunderstand, but also raising such questions as how thoroughly you in fact briefed that person. It is important to learn from the experience; testing what you delegate, to whom, and seeking the best way of handling the process is well worthwhile. If you develop good habits in this area, it can pay dividends over time.

At the end of the day, the effect on others is as important as the effect on you. People carry out with the greatest enthusiasm and care those things for which they have responsibility. In delegating you pass on the opportunity for additional responsibility and you must also pass on with it the authority to act. As has been said, delegation fosters a good working relationship around a team of people. Not least, it produces challenge and, although there are risks, people will normally strive hard to make it work and the failure rate will thus be low. Certainly, the effect on productivity can be marked. But—there is always a but with anything of this sort—it is a process that needs care, determination and perhaps even sacrifice. Delegation is not just a way of getting rid of the things you regard as chores; among the matters most likely to benefit from delegation are almost certainly things you enjoy doing.

The potential rewards cannot be overrated, and the need to make delegation work is therefore strong. Theodore Roosevelt once said: 'The best executive is the one who has sense enough to pick good men to do what he wants done, and the self-restraint enough to keep from meddling with them while they do it.' Sound advice, and for the manager wanting to be a good time manager it is crucial. The two things go together. You cannot be as good at time management if you are a poor delegator. Get both right and you have a major part of the overall management process working for you. This is an area to think on:

- Do you delegate?
- Do you delegate the right things and do it sufficiently often?
- How well does it work?

While the principles reviewed here are important and it is something to be tackled on the right basis, an intention and commitment to making it work are perhaps most important. It may be worth more time to check it out. Perhaps you should consider attending a course on delegating.

SWAP TASKS

Everyone has different skills and different things they get done most quickly and easily. Some of the things you find laborious, a colleague may think a small matter. As everyone is in this position, all you need to do is organize some exchanges. For example, in the sales office of one of clients, two people did this very effectively. One person was very good at the analysis, sorting the untidy returns that came in from the sales team into an ordered set of information. The other was good at presenting the information in graphic form—using software they knew backwards and others did not.

In the official work allocation, they had both been given the complete job to do for different product sales results. In effect, they swapped and all the analysis was done by one, while all the graphic representation was done by the other. The entire job was completed more easily and faster and there was more time to apply to other tasks, primarily dealing with customers, which made up their responsibilities. They felt it was a fair swap in time terms and all worked well.

This is something that can be done in all sorts of ways around groups of people working together, or even in different departments. There is only one snag to watch out for and that is any developmental role that is part of a job having been allocated to someone in the first place. If a manager expects you to become familiar with a task and build up some sort of expertise in it, then you are not likely to do that by letting someone else do the work. That apart, it works well as an idea and you may want to be on the lookout for suitable swap situations that will help you. They must turn out to be fairly balanced, of course—if one party ends up with far more work than the other, then the arrangement will falter, as someone will end up unhappy. More complex swaps, for example two smaller tasks for one larger one, may achieve a suitable balance. Choose well and you may evolve a number of such arrangements all around the organization, all saving you time. As long as the network does not become too complicated (it must continue to work when you are away for a while, and deadlines must be compatible) then it is one more useful way of saving time on a regular basis.

DEVELOP YOUR STAFF

Delegation is one of the greatest opportunities for managers to create more time for themselves. There is one potential snag, however, simply that the people to whom you delegate must have the necessary skill and aptitude to take on delegated tasks and make a good job of them. What their skill level actually is depends largely on you. You recruit and select them, and one of your responsibilities is helping them to develop. Training and development is one of those things that most people agree is a 'good thing', yet it is also something that is all too easy to miss out when you are busy. Here is an additional reason to make sure that it does not get overlooked: help your people develop and they will help you do your job, because not only will the team perform better, but you will be able to delegate more to them.

As a responsible manager, you should have an individual development plan for every single person who reports to you. This will stem in part from their annual appraisal meeting and evaluation, and can usefully include: things that you will do, for example by personal counselling; things they will do, such as private study and experiment and practice; and things that, as it were, the organization will do for them, such as sending them on a course or providing other training resources for them to use.The criteria that decide what development is necessary will arise from an analysis of a person's job, defining what is necessary to do it, then determining whether the person matches up to this or whether there is a skills gap that must be closed by training. In addition, the manager has to look ahead, asking how the job will be different in future because such changes may widen the training gap. Topics for training range wide, but they should include a link with your job as manager and anticipate possible delegation opportunities.

What tasks must you cope with during the next year and what other things might you shed to make room for the new things you have to tackle? The obvious choices for matters to delegate are those that staff can already do competently. But it may well be worth looking more broadly at what possibilities there are if some development is done first. This can be a classic case of a positive balance: time investment is necessary, but the pay-of can often be well worthwhile. It is a pity if the longer-term nature of this process makes it less likely to be taken advantage of because, not only will you save time, but it will also lead to the other advantages of delegation: personal motivation and stimulation to the process of running the organization.

USE TIME-SAVING PHRASE

There is a scene that is played out in offices all over the world and that must waste untold hours every single day. Imagine a manager is busy in his or her office when a head comes round the door and a member of staff comes in. 'What is it?' the manager asks. And the reply is something like: 'I am not sure how to handle such-and-such and wondered if you would just check it with me.' The manager thinks for a second. He or she is busy—in the middle of a job and not wanting to lose concentration—but has already been interrupted. So, his or her first thought is to minimize the interruption and get back to work fast. If the matter allows, the manager spends a minute or two explaining what to do and then tells the other person to let them get on, and the brief impromptu meeting ends. This may be done kindly or abruptly, the effect is much the same, and the one manager may play out the scene many times in a day.

But suppose the same manager is away from the office for a couple of days. In his or her absence, staff face similar situations. If the manager were in, they would go and ask. In the manager's absence, they simply get on with the job. When the manager returns what does he or she find? A chain of disasters? A plethora of wrong decisions and misjudged actions? Rarely. The things the manager would have checked if he or she had been there have been actioned, and not only is no harm done, everything has probably gone perfectly well.

This takes a few minutes, certainly longer than the earlier response, but if they are coping when you are not there to ask, then you will find that when you prompt them they most often come up with a good answer. Then you can say something like: 'That's fine', and away they go to carry on, leaving you to get back to your own work. Now this is not just a better way of dealing with this situation. It is doing something else of very real value: it is teaching them not to interrupt, but rather to have the confidence to think it through for themselves. You have to be insistent about this. It will not work if you make them think it through only when you have more time, and still provide a quick answer when you are busy. Every time—every single time—someone comes through the door with a question about something with which you believe they should be able to deal unaided, you say: 'What do you think you should do?' It must become a catchphrase. And as this practice continues, the message will get home to them, so that if they even start to think of asking you they can hear your likely response in their mind.

If you do this, you will find such questions coming less and less often. You will find that if they do ask, they move straight to the second stage, and come in with two or three thought-out options just wanting you to say which is best. Resist; ask them. The message will stick and, surprise, surprise, you will find you are saving time. What is more, your people will almost certainly get to like it more also, especially if you comment favourably on how well they are doing on the decisions they are making unaided. This is one of the best-tested and useful time savers around—the most time-saving phrase in the language—and all it needs is some persistence and determination. Early on, you may think it is taking too much time, but the investment formula will surely pay of. Exceptions to your consistency will just make the lesson take longer to get over. But this idea really does work in the longer term. Not to operate this way does your people a disservice and allows you to miss out on one of the best time savers managers can find.

DO NOT HOVER

However work has been passed on, whether it is simple work allocation or a job that has been delegated, managers have to give members of their team space to complete the tasks they are working on. There is a temptation, perhaps particularly when a job is first delegated and you worry whether it will be done right, not only to check up but to do so on an ad hoc basis.

Because this is of-putting to those who may be at some mid-point on a job—a point at which things are not finished and look that way—it can actually end up delaying things and perhaps give you a false impression of their capabilities. These checks take time and may set back the way things are going rather than help. Certainly, they do nothing for motivation.

Do not hover. If something needs checking, and it may well do, then such checks should be discussed and agreed at the start of the work. Then the people concerned know what to expect. They can plan for any checks at particular moments and such checks will, as a result, be more likely to be constructive—or indeed unnecessary as those concerned will work to make sure that when the monitoring process arrives all is on schedule. If you work to make such checks an agreed part of the plan, if you make them constructive, then you will not have to spend very much time on them at all. The team working well, with minimal supervision, is a great asset to any manager wanting to conserve his or her own time.

MOTIVATE YOUR STAFF

Motivation is a powerful force. By acting on people's knowledge and ability, it can improve performance, efficiency and productivity—and save time. But, like so much else in management, this does not just happen. Unless you work at it, and that means some time will be taken up, you will not get the best from people, and that means some time will be wasted. Again, the equation of time here makes sense; the net effect should be a saving.

Motivation has been described as a climate and this is not a bad analogy just like the temperature in a room, many different things can affect people's motivation, and the effect can be for good or ill. There is sadly no magic formula for guaranteeing that motivation will be, and will stay, high. You have to look at the motivational implications of things such as the administration and systems with which people work, the way they relate to colleagues and to you as supervisor, and their feeling of security in the sense of knowing what they have to do and being part of a good team. All these can pull motivation down if they are organized badly or unsympathetically.

SPECIFIC TIME MANAGEMENT

People who work together in an office can be infected by the prevailing practices and habits. In an office where some people habitually arrive late in the morning and nothing is said, more people will tend to follow suit and the situation will spread and get worse. This is a negative point, but here I am more concerned with the positive. If you want time management to be an issue that people care about, think about and work at, then you must take the initiative and lead by example. Several practices may be useful here, for example:

- *Set up standard systems.* It is not too dictatorial to set up, and insist on, certain systems that you feel will help everyone's time utilization; for example, the same priority codes used around the office, the same basis for completing diaries (or even the same diary or time system), an insistence on tidy desks—you can probably think of more.
- *Use standard reporting procedures.* Here again a standard helps; such things as memo style, when, where and how meetings are scheduled, notice boards, all can help create a climate of efficiency if they are well organized.
- *Explain.* If you tell people why you do certain things, work in certain ways and why you expect

them to do likewise then it is more likely that, seeing good and personally useful reason, they will comply.

With practice, habits follow and then the time saving around and amongst a group of people accumulates. So, be a public advocate for the virtues of time management, say you believe in it, say you practise it, and do not just expect your team to follow suit—make it easy for them by introducing them to the systems and laying down a few rules to make it all stick. If you help them in these kinds of ways, it will help you too.

KEEP SOME FIRM RULES

The days of dictatorial management have, by and large, long gone. Management in today's environment necessarily involves consultation. It makes sense. People will go along much more wholeheartedly with things—policies, practices, whatever—if they feel they have played some part in their origination. At its most powerful, this creates what is nowadays called ownership and is a force for commitment and getting results. But there are limits just because consultation is a good thing, it does not mean that you have to consult, interminably, over everything. To balance the time this takes, you need other areas where, while the policy is sensibly constituted, there is no debate and no time wasted on it.

There is a firm rule, possibly a sanction, and it is clearly understood that there will be no exceptions, no excuses and no time wasted. If something does go wrong having set up things on this basis, then you have to descend from a great height and read the riot act—and do so consistently.

Such rules provide major time saving. Have a think about the things that go on in your office and amongst your people. You may well have some candidate systems or procedures that are due this sort of treatment. If so, start working on them soon. It is another area that can, in itself, not only save time, but also help to position attitudes and develop the right habits.

SET UP GOOD MEETINGS

It is said that the ideal meeting consists of two people—with one absent! And another saying refers to meetings, bloody meetings. There is truth in both, yet meetings are an important part of organizational communication, consultation and debate. So, this is an important topic to relate to time management, and certainly a major potential cause of time waste.

Whatever the meeting, large or small, formal or informal, long or short, if it is actively planned, considered and conducted to make it go well, then it can be made to work. Meetings have various purposes: to inform, analyse and solve problems, discuss and exchange views, inspire and motivate, counsel and reconcile conflict, obtain opinion and feedback, persuade, train and develop, reinforce the status quo, impress and progress projects in a variety of ways.

You can no doubt expand the list. The key purpose is surely most often to prompt change, and this means making decisions. So any meeting has to be constructive. It must put people in a position where good decisions can prompt appropriate action.

Note also that good meetings are not just useful, they can also stimulate discussion and action that would never occur unless a particular group got together. What makes for a good meeting?

If a meeting is to be truly successful, then ensuring its success cannot begin only as the meeting starts—the 'I think we're all here, what shall we deal with first?'

school of meeting organization. Making it work starts before the meeting, sometimes some time before. First, ask some basic questions, for example:

- Is a meeting really necessary?
- Should it be a regular meeting?
- Who should attend?

If you are clear in these respects then you can proceed. Some key points to bear in mind include:

- *Setting an agenda.* This is very important; no meeting will go as well if you simply make up the content as you get under way.
- *Timing.* Set a start time *and* a finishing time, then you can judge the way it is to be conducted alongside the duration and even put some rough timings to individual items to be dealt with. Respect the timing too: start on time and try to stick with the duration planned.
- *Objective.* Always set a clear objective so that you can say why a meeting is being held.
- *Prepare yourself.* Read all necessary papers, check all necessary details and think about how you will handle both your own contribution and the stimulation, and control, of others.
- *Insist others prepare also.* This may mean instilling habits.
- *People.* Who should be there and what roles individuals should have.
- *Environment. A* meeting will go much more smoothly if people attending are comfortable and uninterrupted.

Then, at the appointed hour, someone must take charge and make the meeting go well.

Leading a Meeting

Even a simple meeting needs someone in the chair. That does *not* imply that whoever it is must be the most senior person present, do most of the talking or even lead the talking, or that they need to be formally called 'chairperson'—but someone must *direct* the meeting. An effective chairperson can ensure a well-directed meeting and in turn means:

- The meeting will better focus on its objectives.
- Discussion can be kept more constructive.
- A thorough review can be assured before ad hoc decisions are taken.
- All sides of the argument or case can be reflected and balanced.
- Proceedings can be kept businesslike and less argumentative.

Thus, all the results of effective chairing are positive, and all allow a meeting to be succinct. To summarize, a good chairperson will lead the meeting, handle the discussion and act to see objectives are met, promptly, efficiently and effectively and without wasting time.

Some of what must be done is simple. Much is common sense; the whole of the role is important. Two simple but key rules that any chairperson must stick to are: only one person may talk at a time and the chairperson decides who (when necessary).

Already all this begins to highlight the qualities of the person who will make a good 'chair'. It is always a vital role. They must command respect, ensure order and ensure that the discussion moves purposefully towards its objectives. They must listen, summarize and, on occasion, pour oil on troubled waters. Effectively they are 'in charge', though this needs to be diplomatically achieved. Finally, consider two other important factors.

Getting of to a Good Start

The best meetings start well, continue well and end well. The chairperson should start the meeting in a way that:

- is positive;
- makes its purpose clear and seen to be businesslike;
- establishes the chairperson's authority and right to be in charge;
- creates the right atmosphere;
- generates interest and enthusiasm for the topics.

It usually helps if the chairperson involves others early on, rather than beginning with a lengthy monologue. This indicates a final point.

Prompting Discussion

Of course, sometimes *prompting* contributions is the least of the problems, but you want contributions from everyone. So, to ensure you get adequate and representative discussion and that subsequent decisions are made on all the appropriate facts you may need to prompt discussion.

Watch for specific reasons for silent participants. For example: they may fear rejection or pressure of other, more senior or more powerful, people, be unprepared, have an incomplete understanding of what has gone before or, indeed, may simply need encouragement. A good chairperson will ask for views and prompt open, considered comments.

Remember tone or manner can easily skew comments. For in stance, someone senior is unlikely to encourage creative suggestions by fielding their own thoughts first: 'It is only a suggestion, but do bear in mind who's making it.' So, do not lead.

In many organizations, meetings are unproductive or unconstructive not because how they are undertaken is ill-considered, but because making them successful is hardly considered at all. There is a real opportunity here. Time spent making sure that meetings do not waste time is time well spent. And careful planning, and attention to necessary detail, will make sure meetings go well and that is even more important. People are major time wasters; but they are also allies in creating productivity.

❖❖❖

7

TIME MANAGEMENT TECHNIQUES

Tme management refers to assigning specific time slots to activities as per their importance and urgency in order to make the best possible use of time. In a layman's language Time Management is nothing but to manage time well and doing things when they actually need to be done.

Let us go through some time management techniques:

— *Set your Priorities. Know what all needs to be done on an urgent basis.* Prepare a "TO DO" List or a "Task Plan" to jot down tasks you need to complete against the time slot assigned to each activity. High Priority Tasks must be written on top followed by tasks which can be done a little later. Make sure you stick to your Task List.

— *Make sure you finish your assignments within the stipulated time frame.* Tick the tasks you have already finished. Treat yourself with a chocolate if you finish your assignments ahead of deadlines.

— *Understand the difference between urgent and important work.* Manage your work well. Do not begin your day with something which is not so important and can be done a little later. First finish off what all is urgent and important. Do not wait for your Boss's reminders.

- *Stay focused.* Do not leave your work station if some urgent work needs to be done. Going for strolls in the middle of an urgent work breaks continuity and an individual tends to loose his focus. Individuals who kill time at work find it difficult to survive workplace stress.
- *Do include time for your tea breaks, net surfing, personal calls and so on in your daily schedule.* It is important. Human being is not a machine who can work at a stretch for eight to nine hours. Assign half an hour to fourty five minutes to check updates on social networking sites, call your friends or family or go for smoke breaks etc.
- *Set realistic and achievable targets for yourself.* Know what you need to achieve and in what duration? Do not lie to yourself. Assigning one hour to a task which you yourself know would require much more time does not make sense.
- *Do not overburden yourself.* Say a firm no to your boss if you feel you would not be able to complete a certain assignment within the assigned deadline. Don't worry, he will not feel bad. Probably he can assign the same to any of your fellow workers. Accept tasks which you are really confident about.
- *Be disciplined and punctual.* Avoid taking unnecessary leaves from work unless there is an emergency. Reach work on time as it helps you to plan your day better.
- *Keep things at their proper places.* Files must be kept at their respective drawers. Staple important documents and put them in a proper folder. Learn to be a little more organized. It will save your time which goes on unnecessary searching.
- *Do not treat your organization as a mere source of money.* Change your attitude. Avoid playing games

on computer or cell phones during office hours. It is unprofessional. Do not work only when your boss is around. Taking ownership of work pays you in the long-run.

- *Develop the habit of using an organizer.* It helps you plan things better. Keep a notepad and a pen handy. Do not write contact numbers or email ids on loose papers. You will waste half of your time searching them. Manage your emails. Create separate folders for each client. Do not clutter your desktop.

HOW TO PRACTICE EFFECTIVE TIME MANAGEMENT IN ORGANIZATION?

Every organization works on deadlines. An individual constantly needs to be on his toes to finish off assignments within stipulated time frame. It is essential for employees to understand the value of time for them to do well and make a mark of their own at the workplace.

- *Know your targets well.* Do not hesitate to speak to your Boss if targets are unrealistic and unachievable within the allocated time slot. It is always better to discuss things at the initial stages than cutting a sorry figure later on. Accept tasks only when you are confident.
- *There is absolutely no harm in discussing work with your fellow workers.* You can't do almost everything on your own. Distribute work amongst your team members. It is foolish to over burden yourself. One must share his work load with others to finish assignments within the stipulated time frame. Know your capabilities.
- *Organize yourself.* Be very careful about your files, important documents, visiting cards, folders etc.

Keep them at their proper places so that you do not waste half of your time in searching them.

- *Be loyal to your organization.* Do not work only when your superiors are around. Remember you are getting paid for your hard work. Concentrate on your own work rather than loitering and gossiping around. Do not waste time by playing games on computer or finding out what your fellow worker is up to.
- *Plan your things well in advance.* Do not work just for the sake of working. The first thing an employee should do in the morning is to jot down what all tasks he need to do in a single day against the time slot assigned to each task. Preparing a Task Plan right at the start of the day always helps and provides you a sense of direction at work. A "TO DO" List suggests you way forward. Tick off completed assignments. Make sure you finish tasks within the assigned deadlines.
- *Keep a notepad and pen handy.* Avoid writing on loose papers. You will never find them when you actually need something. Prefer using an organizer as it helps you plan your work better.
- *Eat only during lunch hours.* Eating while working not only makes you feel sleepy but also breaks continuity.
- *Be punctual.* Avoid taking frequent leaves from work unless it is an emergency. Make it a habit to reach office on time.
- *Do not keep things pending at your end.* Escalate matters immediately which need approval of higher authorities. Do not keep ignoring things. They would create problems for you sooner or later.

8

TIME MANAGEMENT CHALLENGES

MANAGING INTERRUPTIONS

Everyday interruptions at work can be a key barrier to managing your time effectively and, ultimately, can be a barrier to your success.Think back to your last workday, and consider for a minute the many interruptions that occurred. They may have been phone calls, emails, hallway converzations, colleagues stopping by your office, or anything else that unexpectedly demanded your attention and, in doing so, distracted you from the task at-hand.

Because your day only has so many hours in it, a handful of small interruptions can rob you of the time you need to achieve your goals and be successful in your work and life. More than this, they can break your focus, meaning that you have to spend time re-engaging with the thought processes needed to successfully complete complex work.The key to controlling interruptions is to know what they are and whether they are necessary, and to plan for them in your daily schedule. The tips that follow will help you do that, and so prevent interruptions from frustrating you and jeopardizing your success.

Using the Tool

Use the following tips to understand and manage interruptions:

Keep an Interrupters Log

If interruptions consistently rob you of time and energy, or if they frequently push you off schedule and cause delays, it's time to keep an Interrupters Log. This is a simple record of the interruptions you experience in the course of a day.

Person	Date and Time	Description of Interruption	Valid?	Urgent?

Figure 1: The Interrupters Log

Keep your Interrupters Log with you every day for at least a week, recording every interruption you experience, and marking down the person interrupting you; the date and time it occurs; what the interruption is; whether it was valid; and whether it was urgent (or whether someone could have waited until a better time.) Once you have recorded the interruptions for a week, sit down with your log and analyse the information. Which interruptions are valid and which are not? You need to deal with the valid interruptions. We'll show you below how you can schedule them into your day so that they get the attention they need, while you still have the time you need to adequately address your daily work. As for the interruptions that are not valid, you must find a way to block these out in the future.

Analyse and Conquer Interruptions

To analyse and conquer the interruptions you find in your Interrupters Log, firstly look at whether the interruption is valid or not. Could someone have avoided interrupting you by waiting for a routine meeting? Or was it something they should have asked you about at all? If not, deal with this politely but assertively.

Next, look at how urgent the interruptions were, and whether they could have been pre-empted. You can pre-empt many interruptions by holding routine meetings with people: If they're confident that they'll have access to you at a defined point in the near future, they'll learn to save up non-urgent issues until this meeting. However, some interruptions are both urgent and valid. You need to be interrupted, and you need to deal with the situation.

From your Interrupters Log, you'll see how much time is taken up by these urgent, valid interruptions. Block this time into your schedule as "contingency time", and only take on as much other work as you can fit into the remaining time. You'll have to juggle this other work around the interruptions, but at least you won't be overloaded and stressed by the things that you haven't done because they've been displaced by emergencies.

Put Your Phone to Work for You (Not Against You)

A little bit of planning can go a long way in working to control telephone interruptions, which many people experience all day long. If you are on a deadline or your focus needs to be intense (and not interrupted), use your voice mail to screen calls, or have an assistant deal with messages for you. This way, you can deal with calls by priority, and at times that suit you. In fact, this telephone time can be planned into your schedule, and so become a normal part of your working day.

Catch Your Breath

When interrupted, it's easy to get caught up in the "rush" of the person who is interrupting, for they undoubtedly feel their request is urgent. In reality, however, most interruptions are not genuinely crisis-driven, and it can serve everyone best to take a little time before taking action. Take a few minutes to consider the situation. Catch your breath and clear your head. A small delay, even one of just a few minutes, goes a long way in assessing the situation accurately and reacting appropriately.

Learn to Say "No"

It's often acceptable to say "no" to requests or tasks if you are busy when someone else can handle it, if it is not an important task, or if it can be done later. When this is the case, saying "no" in a courteous and sincere way, followed by a short explanation is the best course of action to take: "I am working against a very tight deadline on an important project right now so, I am sorry, but I can not jump in and help".

"Available" and "Unavailable" Time

Simple yet effective: Let people know when you are available. and when you are not. Make sure that people know that during your "unavailable time", they should only interrupt you if they have to. You and your co-workers can also agree on a signal that everyone in the office can use when unavailable, like turning the nameplate on the door around, or simply closing the door. This alleviates interruptions and can avoid hurt feelings.

Be careful here. If you're a manager, an important part of your job is to be available to people, to handle urgent issues which arise, and to coach your team so that people are as effective as possible. If you put up barriers that are too high, you won't be able to do these jobs. By all means, use "unavailable time", but don't over use it, and make sure people know they can interrupt you if there is a genuine crisis.

"Invitation Only" Time

Schedule regular check-in times for the individuals you talk to most often. Ask these people to keep a running list of things that they need to discuss, so you can cover all the points at one time. And, force yourself to do the same. An open-door policy is good, but you should limit the number of people you invite to your work area. For instance, if you're scheduling a meeting, offer to meet your co-worker in his or her office or a conference room. This way, you can excuse yourself after you accomplish your purpose. Additionally, it's much easier to get up and leave than it is to get people to leave your office once they're seated and comfortable.

Uncontrollable Interruptions

There are interruptions that, no matter how hard you try, you simply cannot control. Most people are happy to schedule a more convenient time, but when this does not work, quickly set the parameters by saying something like, "I only have five minutes to talk about this right now," and stick to it. Do not ask the interrupter to sit down and do not engage in small talk. Encourage the interrupter to get right to the point and if a solution cannot be reached before the allotted time runs out, set a time for getting back to them and, again, stick to it.

DEALING WITH LATENESS

Do you have a colleague who regularly arrives late for meetings? It's an annoying habit, and it's even worse if everyone else must wait for him because he's a key person in the decision-making process. Or perhaps you have a colleague who frequently turns up late at the office, complaining about "nightmare traffic" on her drive to work. Worse still, are you the person who is always late? Lateness is bad for team productivity or team morale, and it may point to a wider lack of responsibility. So, what can you do to stop it? Sometimes the causes will be obvious. Other times, the reason for habitual lateness can be rooted in the person's subconscious.

Whoever the habitual latecomer is, identifying why the lateness occurs is the first step toward eliminating it. Sometimes the causes will be obvious. Other times, the reason for habitual lateness can be rooted in the person's subconscious.

Change the behaviour, not the employee—if you can

If six guys on the night shift punch in late at the Honda plant, it's not going to cause the automaker much grief. If employees of a small business decide to sleep in or take a "mental health day," it can be a disaster. Think about the contractor who depends on a construction crew to complete a project on a tight deadline or the printer who relies on his service reps to answer urgent client questions.

Chronic lateness is not a trivial matter. Tardy employees delay production if you're a manufacturing company, create customer problems if you're in retail, and trigger morale problems for the staff who come in on time.

As maddening as chronic lateness can be, however, employers need to keep a cool head when looking for a solution. The goal should be to fix the behaviour, not eliminate the employee. It's always costly to hire and train new workers and, with unemployment at 4.5% nationally, in many parts of the country it can take weeks or months to find a new hire.

If employees are late, they know they that there are consequences. Depending on how late they are, an Amercian company deducts a half hour or hour from their paychecks and reduces their weekly bonus, which is based on daily sales goals and also includes incentives for additional sales. The company has created a checklist of penalties: First time late draws a warning, second time the bonus is cut by Rs.500, third time by Rs. 2000 and fourth time no bonus. It considered offering bonuses for being on time, but she thinks rewarding staff for doing their job isn't a good idea. The system hasn't eliminated tardiness, but it reduces the wear and tear on the boss.

But letting some employees get away with breaking the rules—even if they are paying penalties—can be bad for the organization. If an employee has had adequate warnings and the boss has made it clear that this behavior is hurting the business, the boss may need to follow through with dismissal. Firing an employee sends a clear signal.

The above said compant did the right thing was in establishing written policies. Too many small businesses are reluctant to "go corporate" and fail to establish formal policies about absenteeism and tardiness. That is a mistake because boundaries must be set in writing. Making the rules clear and spelling out penalties helps employers and employees. Policies should be written down and distributed to employees when they are hired so there are no questions about what the boss expects.

Of course, it helps not to hire chronically late employees in the first place. Most small business owners fail to call references. But if you did, you could ask how reliable was the employee? How often was he late in the last month? Past behavior is the best predictor of future behaviour. Asking these questions is permissible and doesn't any break any laws, though past employers have a right not to answer them.

Lateness has seldom been a problem because everything is done as a team and peer pressure exerts influence on workers to get in on time. If one worker is late and the project is delayed, the team suffers. If lateness occurs several times, supervisors deal with the issues during performance appraisals.

If an employee who has always showed up on time starts to arrive late, don't let it slide—ask what has changed. Lateness can be a symptom that they don't like their job or are having a problem at home. Consider contacting your healthcare provider, which may offer Employee Assistance Programs, which can help employees who are having personal problems.

Be flexible—where you can be. If an employee can't get to work at 8:30 a.m., maybe a 10 a.m. to 7 p.m. shift would be more productive for her.

Think positive: Team rewards can reinforce on-time behaviour. Scott says a contracting firm he knows posts a chart, recording when each member of a five-man crew shows up. If they rack up a perfect on-time record for the week, the manager takes the team out to dinner Friday night as a reward. "Peer pressures helps to get everyone in on time," she notes.

MANAGING YOUR WORK ENVIRONMENT

How often are you distracted at work?It's a question that's almost laughable, right? Most of us are distracted several times, if not dozens of times, every day. We get emergency emails and phone calls. We take breaks to browse the Internet. Co-workers walk into our office for a quick chat, or send us amusing instant messages.It doesn't matter where you work or what you do, you probably deal with distractions on a daily basis. What's more (and depending on the complexity of our work), regaining concentration after a distraction can take quite a few minutes. If we're distracted 10 times a day, multiply the time lost by 10, and it's easy to see why we sometimes don't get much quality work done.Learning how to minimize distractions can dramatically increase your productivity and effectiveness, as well as reduce your stress. Without distractions, you can get into flow, produce high-quality work, and achieve much more during the day.

Email

While email is incredibly useful, it's also one of the biggest work distractions we face. Many of us could spend entire days simply reading and responding to emails.

- *Schedule "email" times*—Minimize this distraction by scheduling specific times to check and respond to emails. For instance, you could check email when you first arrive at work, at lunch, and right before you leave, and specify a half-hour slot every day to respond to your emails. (If you do this, it may be useful to let co-workers and customers know that they will need to contact you another way if they need you urgently.)
- *Check and respond to email at "low productivity" times* —Remember that there are certain times of day when you probably do your best work. Some people work best in the morning, and others late at night. Schedule your email check-in during your less-productive times—and save your peak hours for doing creative, high-value work.

- *Turn emails into actions*—If an email will take more than a few minutes to action or respond to, add it as a new action on your To-Do List or Action Programme.
- *Keep your email programme closed*—When you're not using your email programme, close it entirely—or at least turn off the visual or audible alerts that distract you. This eliminates the temptation to check it constantly.

Most email programmes will also allow you to fetch new email manually with a "send/receive" button, or will allow you to set it to get new email automatically at certain times of the day.

Disorganization

A disorganized desk or office can be very distracting. When your work space or work life is disorganized, it can be difficult to think and plan clearly. Getting organized is a topic that could easily fill books, and it does!

Imagine this scenario: After a week of hard work, you send an important report to your colleague. His task is to edit the wording and make a few key decisions to finalise some of the content. The deadline is still three weeks away, but you hope he'll finish it early because you'll have more work to do once he gives you his input. Your colleague, however, delays making the changes. After numerous reminders from you, he sends it back the day before your deadline. This means that you have to rush to complete your final changes in time. His delay has caused you some serious stress, and it's not the first time that this has happened.Working with disorganized people can be a stressful experience, especially when it starts impacting your own productivity. But what can you do about it? Is it your responsibility to help them get organized? If yes, how do you do it tactfully? Whether they're colleagues, team members, or even your manager, we'll explore strategies to help you to help them.

Instant Messaging (IM)

Instant messaging can be useful, but many times it's also a way for co-workers to interrupt you without having to get up and walk into your office. If you use instant messaging (it's very powerful if used in a disciplined way), get into the habit of using it for small, quick queries. It's often better to use email or the phone for more complex ones. Also, if you find yourself distracted by IM, consider setting specific times during the day for being "online." Then, when you don't want to be contacted, leave it off or set your status to "busy." If people need to contact you, make sure they know your "hours" for IM.

Phone Calls

The ring of the phone has become almost like Pavlov's bell for some people—we think we must answer it, even if we're concentrating on something important. Minimize phone call distractions by turning off your phone during your peak work hours. Or, let your team know that you won't take non-essential calls between specific times, such as from noon to 2 pm. Alternatively, get people into the habit of using IM to check with co-workers that they are OK to take a call. If co-workers are deep in concentration, they can ask to "talk in 10 minutes" without losing the thread of their work.

The Internet

Browsing the web can take up enormous amounts of time from our day, and when we start looking on the Internet for one thing, it's easy to get lost for 20 minutes or more.

- *Read the news before the start of the day*–Visit news sites or read newspapers before work, so that you know the news. That way, you won't be distracted as much during the day.
- *Close your Internet browser*–Eliminate Internet distractions by keeping your browser closed when you're not using it. If you repeatedly check personal email, or go on social networking sites like Facebook or Twitter, then log out of your account. If you're forced to take those few extra seconds to log in each time, it may remind you that you're not focusing on work.
- *Use special software*–There are some useful software applications such as Freedom and Anti-Social that help eliminate online distractions. You can specify which websites you want to block, and set a timer for how long you want the block to remain active. Using technology like this to block access for yourself can be a big help.
- *Take short Internet breaks*–Remember that taking little breaks, especially after working for an hour or more in deep concentration, can be quite useful for resting your mind. These tiny breaks allow you to return to focus with renewed energy. Use casual Internet browsing as a reward for every hour you devote to high-quality, focused work – and you'll feel as if you've earned the time.

Other People

Co-workers often create the greatest distractions.

- *Close your door*–Close your office door to keep people from casually stopping by. If they knock or come in anyway, explain that when your door is closed, you shouldn't be disturbed unless there's an emergency. A sign on your office door may also help.

- *Use headphones*–If you're in a cubicle or open office environment, people are less likely to interrupt you if you're wearing headphones.
- *Talk to the disrupter*–If you share an office with someone who often disrupts your day, talk to the person about the problem: he may not realise he's distracting you. Or, if a co-worker often comes in, sits down, and chats for a while, don't allow her to do it—place a pile of papers on the chair she'd use, or stand up immediately when she comes into your office or cubicle.

Work Environment

Windows, a busy highway, or loud co-workers may all contribute to a distracting work environment.

- *Work in another location*–If possible, work in a conference room or empty office to regain your concentration. If your job allows it, working in a different setting, such as at home, at a library, or in a coffee shop, may also help you to focus more.
- *Use "white noise"*–If noise is a problem, install padded partitions, or consider buying a sound machine that produces white noise to cover annoying sounds. Noise-canceling headphones with soft music can also improve your focus. You can also download white noise files from the Internet and set them on "repeat." Having white noise play constantly helps block unwanted sounds.

Other Projects and Tasks

- An overwhelming To-Do List may be a major distraction during the day. You may then procrastinate on those tasks, simply because you have so much to do, which further lowers your productivity.

- *Prioritise your To-Do List*—Commit to accomplishing the two most important tasks on your list every day.
- *Track your day*—Pick one day to keep track of everything you spend your time doing. You might discover that you spend five hours managing interruptions and dealing with emergencies, and four hours doing actual work. This assessment would then show you that you have only four productive hours each day to achieve your most important tasks.
- *Delegate*—Learn how to delegate effectively. This is important for managing an overwhelming list of tasks and projects.

Tiredness

Coming to work well rested is vital to having a productive day.

- *Get enough slee*—Many people don't get enough sleep at night. When you're tired, it's very easy to become distracted.
- *Stay hydrated*—When you don't drink enough water and you become dehydrated, you may not think clearly. Dehydration can also make you feel tired and less alert. Keep a water bottle on your desk, and drink regularly during the day.
- *Go for a walk*—If you're tired at work, go outside for a walk. Getting some fresh air and moving your body can give you more energy, and can make you feel more alert.
- *Watch your diet*—Your diet may also influence how tired you feel. For example, avoid heavy lunches – and instead eat smaller, healthy snacks throughout the day.

The Art of Concise Converzations

Does this sound familiar? One of your colleagues phones you for advice about her project. However, instead of getting right to the point, she spends 20 minutes telling you about her son's latest baseball game, your boss's recent promotion, and the office manager's new shoes. Or even worse, there's your co-worker who makes a point, and then spends the next half hour saying it over and over in several different ways – or he keeps going over the same conclusions you've both already agreed on. It seems like your clothes will go out of style before the converzation ends. Have you been in situations like these? The business world (and the world in general) is filled with people who don't seem to know how to stick to the subject. This not only affects your working relationships, it can also waste a lot of your time. However, it's important to build relationships with your colleagues. A lot of this happens in unstructured converzations – the same converzations that may be considered "time wasters."

Creating Time in Your Day

Time—it's something that money can't really buy, and something that many of us would like more of! And, with the breakneck pace of work today far outweighing what we had to contend with even a few decades ago, many of us could achieve so much more with a little more time on our hands. With these, you can get more done at work, or spend time doing more of things that you enjoy. It's unlikely that every one of these strategies will fit your own circumstances. However, some of these strategies are sure to help!

9

EFFECTIVE TIPS FOR TIME MANAGEMENT

Time is a resource like any other. And an important one, respect for which can boost effectiveness and profitability—so time management is a crucial skill. It can enhance personal productivity, allow you to focus on priorities, and ultimately act directly to improve your effectiveness and hence the overall success of the organization. Little things do mount up. Saving five minutes may not sound like much use; however, do so every working day in the year and you save nearly two and a half days!

Habits are powerful. Those that need changing may take some effort to shift, but once new ones are established, then they make the approaches they prompt at least semi-automatic. The process of getting to grips with managing your time effectively may well take a conscious effort, but by establishing good working habits it is one that gets easier as you go on. Perhaps nothing provides a better example of wasted time than business meetings, especially internal ones.

The principles of good time management are not complex. Overall they can be summarized in three principles:

- List the tasks you have to perform.
- Assign them priorities.
- Do what the plan says.

It is the last of these principles that causes problems—and, to some extent, the second as well. The logic is usually clear. For example, in conducting training on presentational skills I am regularly told by participants that there is never enough time to prepare. Yet this is a key task. Skimp the preparation, make a lackluster presentation, and weeks of time and work may go down the drain. Putting the preparation time in the diary, setting aside a clear couple of hours or whatever it takes, and sticking to that in a way that avoids interruptions must be worth while.

Yes, such an approach demands some discipline—more if it is a team presentation and colleagues must clear time to be together— but it can be done, and again it pays dividends.

It is a prime principle of time management that time must be invested to save time in the future. Sound preparation of the presentation may take two hours, but how long is involved in replacing a prospect if a sales presentation to a customer goes wrong? No contest. And the same principle applies to systems; sorting something out so that it works well on a regular basis is also likely to be time well spent.

The last of the three main principles above is the one that needs most effort.

There are two main influences that combine to keep you from completing planned tasks. The first is other people and events, and the second is you—procrastination, and interruptions, are ever present. So what helps with all this and keeps you on track? Sadly, there is no magic formula: no one thing that can be done to turn you into a master time manager.

Success is in a number of details; what makes for the best situation is when your overall attitude makes many of these—in one form or another—into habits. The ideas here add up to a complete solution, but they are all valuable in their own right, and those that suit you can be adopted one at a time.

Good time management is a real asset to anyone's productivity and effectiveness. Its good effects and habit can proliferate through a team, a company even, and there is clearly a direct link between personal effectiveness and the achievement of corporate objectives. The potential good effects are positive and broad in their impact. So it is worth exploring the possibilities, instilling the right habits, and avoiding any dilution of your firm intentions.

Some effective tips for good time management are described below. Many of these ideas are no doubt in use by many different people. Almost every tips documented here can be useful to most executives and managers—it is their usefulness that got them included.

1. SEE WHERE TIME GOES NOW

Any improvement you may be able to make to your time utilization must surely presuppose that you know where time goes in the way that you work now. Most people define this inaccurately unless they check it out.

There are two ways to check current practice. The first is to estimate it—guesstimate it might be a better phrase. This is most easily done in percentage terms on a simple pie chart. Decide on the main categories of work that define your job and divide the pie chart into segments. Such categories might include:

- Writing.
- Telephoning.

— Meetings.

— Planning.

And they could be more personal: so in case they would span specific activities such as conducting training and writing books.

The second way is to use a time log to obtain a much more accurate picture—recording everything you do through the day and doing so for at least a week, longer if you can.

2. PLAN, WORK— WORK, PLAN

The wise saying that you should "plan the work, and work the plan" was mentioned in the introduction. Certainly any real progress with time management needs a plan. This must be in writing and must be reviewed and updated regularly; for most people this means a daily check.

To repeat, the idea here is simply to have a written plan and regularly check and update it. What is needed is thus sometimes called a rolling plan; not only is it updated regularly, it also provides a snapshot of your workload ahead at any particular moment. As such, it should show accurately and completely your work plan for the immediate future, and give an idea of what lies beyond. As you look ahead, there will be some things that are clear a long way forward—for example, when an annual budget must be prepared and submitted; other areas are less clear and, of course, much cannot be anticipated at all in advance.

At its simplest, such a plan is just a list of things to do. It may include:

— A daily plan.

— A weekly plan.

- Commitments that occur regularly (weekly or monthly or annually).
- A plan for the coming month (perhaps linked to a planning chart).

The exact configuration will depend on the time span across which you work. What is important is that it works for you, that it is clear, that different kinds of activity show up for what they are, and that everything links clearly to your diary and appointment system.

One point here is crucial. Some people, perhaps most, have a proportion of their day in which action is reactive. Things occur that cannot be predicted, at least individually, and a proportion of the available time is always going to go in this way. Such activity is not automatically unimportant, and the reverse may well be true. For example, a manager on the sales or marketing side of a commercial company may have inquiries and queries coming from customers that are very important and must be dealt with promptly, but will nevertheless make fitting in everything else more difficult. Sometimes the reaction to this is to believe that, because of this reactive element, it is not possible to plan, or to plan effectively. The reverse is true. If your days do consist, even in part, of this sort of random activity, it is even more important to plan, because there is inherently less time available to do the other things that the job involves and that time has to be planned even more thoroughly to maximize its effectiveness.

Everyone needs a plan, everyone can benefit from having a clear view of what there is to be done. If you do not have this, then the work of setting it up will take a moment, but it is worth while and, as has been said, it need not then take long to keep up to date. Once it is in place, you can evolve a system that suits you and that keeps up with the way in which your job and its responsibilities change over time.

3. SETTING CLEAR OBJECTIVES

Any plan is, in turn, as good as the objectives that lie behind it. So it is to objectives, certainly a fundamental factor affecting the management of time, that we now turn.

Always set objectives. Maxims advocating setting clear objectives are everywhere—for example, the idea that if you don't know where you are going any road will do. You do need clear objectives, and they must not be vague or general hopes.

A much quoted acronym spells out the principles involved: objectives should be Smart, that is: Specific, Measurable, Achievable, Realistic, and Timed. An example will help make this clear.

It is all too easy to define the objectives for a workshop on this topic as being simply to ensure participants "make better presentations," a statement that is unlikely to be sufficiently clear to be really useful. Applying the formula might produce a statement such as:

Objectives for a presentation skills course:

- *Specific*: To enable participants to make future presentations in a manner and style that will be seen as appropriate by their respective audiences, and that will enhance the message they put over and allow them to achieve their purpose.
- *Measurable*: In other words, how will we know this has been achieved? Ultimately, in this case by the results of future presentations; but we might also consider that the trainer or the group, or both, will be able to judge this to a degree at the end of the event by observing the standard during practice.
- *Achievable*: Can this be done? The answer in this case will depend on the prevailing standard before the course. If the people are inexperienced and

their standard of presentation is low, then the answer may be that it cannot.

- *Realistic*: Picking up the last point, if the time, say, is inadequate, then the objectives may not be realistic. These people can potentially be improved, we might say, but not in one short session.
- *Timed*: "Timed" in training terms will reflect the timing of the course; it may be scheduled to take place in one month's time, so the objectives cannot, by definition, be realized before then. Also the duration: is a one- or two-day (or any other number of days) program going to do the job?

Such an approach is far more likely to provide guidance in the form of clear objectives. Clear objectives really are important, and any lack of clarity can affect every aspect of a person's work, not least time management, sometimes doing so surreptitiously.

Much of what needs to be done to manage time effectively is concerned with tackling conflicts and making decisions about what comes first, and none of this is possible if there is no underlying clarity about objectives to act as a reference.

This is not the place for a detailed review of objectives setting; suffice it to say that this is important to everything in corporate life. An organization functions best with clear corporate objectives, the management structure works best when individual managers are clear about what it is they are expected to achieve and, in turn, they can get the best from staff if they provide clear objectives for them. Consider your own position. Are there any areas that are not clear in this respect? If so, do they make for problems or conflict regarding the way you go about the job? If you answered "yes" to the first question, then you probably did the same for the second.

Even a simple example makes the point. If a manager is asked to review a system of some sort, it might be for many reasons: to improve accuracy, to speed up operations, to save money, or all three. But undertaking this task is going to take longer if any of this is unclear. In that case, either time needs to be spent working out or checking objectives, or work is put in toward some arbitrary objective that proves inadequate; both end up taking up more time. As it is with one task, so it is with the job overall. If you do not have a clear job description, or if you are uncertain what objectives you should be aiming toward achieving, then check, seek clarification, and managing what you do will at once be easier.

4. SPECULATE TO ACCUMULATE

A further point, again one touched on in the introduction, needs stating as a useful overall principle. You will find that some ways of saving time, or better utilising it, do need an investment—but it is an investment of time. It seems like a contradiction in terms, having to spend time to save time. Again this can all too easily become a barrier to action. Yet the principle is clear.

Invest time to save time: there is a time equation that can and must be put to work if time is to be brought under control. There are many ways of ensuring that time is utilized to best effect, and, while some take only a moment, others take time either to set up or for you to adopt the habit of working in a particular way.

It is quicker to do it yourself. But beware, because this may only be true at the moment something occurs. Say someone telephones you requesting certain information, it doesn't matter what, but imagine that you must locate and look something up, compose a brief comment to explain it, and send the information off to the other person with a note of the comment. It is a minor matter and will take you only four or five minutes.

Imagine further that, to avoid the task, you consider letting someone else do it. They are well able to, but explaining and showing them what needs to be done will certainly take 10–15 minutes of both your time and theirs. It really is quicker to do it yourself. Not so; or rather certainly not so if it is a regularly occurring task. Say it is something that happens half a dozen times a week. If you take the time to brief someone, then they will only have to take the action for less than a week and the time spent briefing will have paid off; thereafter you save a significant amount of time every week, indeed you save time on every occasion that similar requests are made on into the future. This is surely worth while. The time equation here of time spent as a ratio of time saved works positively. This is often the case and worthwhile savings can be made by applying this principle, both to simple examples such as that just stated and to more complex matters where hours or days spent on, say, reorganizing a system or process may still pay dividends.

It is so easy to fall into this trap. For whatever reason, we judge it to be possible (better?) to pause from what we are presently doing for the few moments necessary to get another task out of the way, but not for longer in order to carry out a briefing or whatever other action would rid of the task altogether, and ultimately make a real time saving. It is worth a thought. Become determined not to be caught in this time trap and you are en route to saving a great deal of time.

5. USING PARETO'S LAW

Working effectively means deciding the relative priorities of different tasks. Obvious perhaps, and of course you may say some things are clearly more important than others. But it is very easy to underestimate just how much this concept influences what you need to do, indeed just how much it influences your inherent effectiveness.

Many years ago, the Italian economist Vilfredo Pareto recognized the truism that carries his name and that is now more commonly called the 80/20 rule. It links cause and effect in a ratio and, although this is not represented absolutely accurately in real life, an approximate 80/20 ratio is consistently found in many business activities, sometimes with a precision that is considerable. This means that for instance:

- 20 per cent of a company's customers are likely to produce 80 per cent of its revenue.
- 20 per cent of factory errors are likely to cause 80 percent of quality rejects.

And it applies specifically in terms of issues relating directly to time:

- 20 per cent of meeting time results in about 80 percent of decisions made.
- 20 per cent of items to read that pass across your desk produce 80 per cent of the information you need in your work.

So you must recognize that just 20 percent of your working time probably contributes around 80 per cent of what is necessary for success in your job, and you must reflect this in the way you operate so that attention is focused on those key issues that have this dramatic effect.

Have a look at your job description, at how you spend time, and make yourself think through and decide just what it is about what you do that has the greatest effect. It may not always be obvious for all sorts of reasons. You may take some key things for granted; for instance, forgetting once they have become a routine how important they are. Certainly you are unlikely to find a direct relationship between such a list of key issues and the things that you spend the most time on. Just this simple review may prompt you to make some changes to your work pattern. Clear objectives and a clear job specification, together with a clear idea of which tasks influence what results and which are key in 80/20 terms, are the only rational bases for deciding priorities. Give yourself this basis and you will be better equipped to work effectively both in terms of time spent on key issues and in terms of reducing or eliminating corresponding minor matters.

Given the right intention, and motivation, it is possible for anyone to improve their time utilization, and perhaps for those who have not given any aspect of time management much conscious thought of late to markedly improve the way they work. However, it takes more than a review of time management and the adoption of one or two ideas to make you truly productive for life. The best time managers have not only instilled in themselves good habits and so put part of the process on automatic pilot, as it were; they also view time management as an area of perpetual fine-tuning. In everything they do, the time dimension is considered. It becomes a prerequisite for the various ways in which they work, and they continuously strive to improve still further the way they work and what it allows them to achieve. That fine-tuning too becomes a habit.

6. TACKLING THE TYRANNY OF THE URGENT VERSUS THE IMPORTANT

It can sometimes be curiously difficult to decide certain priorities. Asking why brings to the vexed question of the urgent versus the important. The urgent and the important are different in nature, yet both generate pressure to deal with them "before anything else."

It may help to think here of four categories—things that are:

- — Urgent and important.
- — Important but not urgent.
- — Urgent but not important.
- — Neither important nor urgent.

Overall, the key is to think first and make considered decisions before letting particular circumstances push you into doing anything first, or just trying to do everything. Things that need action taking fast you must then either do, or delegate, at once. Things that will wait should not just be put on one side, but scheduled so that they get the time they deserve and are also completed.

The principle described above may seem difficult; indeed, it *is* difficult. But the difficulty is, at least in part, psychological. We usually know what is most in need of action, yet somehow the pressures of circumstances combine to give some things an "unfair"—and inappropriate—advantage and we allow that to dictate the decision and give something priority. This is a prime area where resolve is more important than technique, where there is no magic formula, and making the right judgments in a considered way must become a habit if we are to remain organized in the face of such pressures.

7. GIVE CLEAR INSTRUCTIONS

There is an old saying that there is never time to do anything properly, but there must always be time to do it again. Nothing is more likely to end up with something having to be redone than a manager not making it clear to people what they had to do in the first place. Communication is not easy, but the responsibility for getting it right is with the communicator—and that, if you are issuing instructions, is you. Similarly, if people do not really understand and fail to query it, perhaps because they are worried you will blame them, then that is also your fault because you should make sure things are clear and encourage people to ask if necessary.

Always ensure that instructions are clear. People should be told:

- *What* needs to be done (and give them sufficient details).
- *Why* it needs to be done (knowing the objectives may make the task clearer and will improve motivation).
- *How* it should be done (methodology etc.).
- *When* it should be completed (and anything else about the timing).

Instructions should always include asking if everything is clear—get some feedback. Any short cut of this sequence must be on the basis of genuine knowledge or familiarity, not simply assumption that all will be well. Good, clear instructions save time, written guidelines do the same, and for some tasks they are useful; this is especially true of awkward or difficult jobs that are performed regularly but infrequently.

One such job in office is changing the toner unit on the laser printer: no one remembers exactly how to do it next time it is necessary, and retaining and consulting the instructions saves time. Moral: all instructions, in whatever form, must be clear. If you issue instructions, remember this; if you receive them—ask if necessary.

8. BEWARE FAVOURITES

This may seem an odd one, but it is potentially even more time-wasting than putting off things that you do not like or that you find difficult. Many people spend a disproportionate amount of time on the things they like doing best and, perhaps, also do best. This is perfectly natural and there are various reasons for it. An important one is that any concentration on what you like is what seems to produce the most job satisfaction. This is fine if that satisfaction comes simply from doing whatever it is and the thing itself is necessary, though the danger is that you may be prone to some over-engineering, doing more than is necessary, putting in more time and sometimes producing a standard of quality or excellence that is just not necessary.

But there can be more sinister reasons for this practice. For example, it may be because:

- You are using one task to provide an excuse to delay or avoid others (difficult or unfamiliar things, perhaps), telling yourself, with seeming reason, that you are too busy to get to them.
- You are concerned about delegating (a subject covered separately) and worry that a task is not a candidate for this, so you go on doing it yourself and go on over-engineering.
- You find the work conditions of one task too tempting, such as a low-priority job that involves visiting an attractive location new to you, for instance; this is something that is compounded by the opposite being true of the priority task.
- You find some aspect of the task fun; as an example, this happens to some people who have a fascination with computers, and they spend hours devising, say, a graphic representation of some figures when something simpler would meet the case just as well.

Avoid what is sometimes called "cherry picking." The answer here is to really look, and look honestly, as you review your tasks and your regular work plan for examples of this happening. Better still, look for examples of where it might happen and make sure that it does not.

Self-generated interruptions can be surprisingly time-consuming and their frequency can be one of the surprises that often emerge from keeping a personal time log. It is easy to be blind to them and, at the risk of being repetitive, it is logical to watch for these before the ones involving other people or outside circumstances as their cause.

9. USE A "DOCUMENT PARKING" SYSTEM

Many of them do not need action, or rather nothing can be done immediately. Such items are what so often constitute the ever-present pending tray that makes many a desk groan under its weight. The net result is that you spend a great deal of time either shuffling through the heap to locate things, or checking things in there to see what you might in time do about them.

The nature of some of the material makes the problem worse. Say one item can only be dealt with when certain monthly performance figures are published; in that case, to keep checking may well be both time-consuming and useless, as no action can be taken until a later stage anyway. Further, constant reviewing can achieve little in advance of knowing what the figures say, as there are many different possibilities in terms of what they might predicate.

If you suffer this sort of situation, you need a parking place for such things, somewhere safe yet guaranteed to trigger prompt action at the appropriate moment. You need what is called a Prompt File. This means you take an item and decide when you will be able to progress it. This may be at a specific time, or it may not. Then you simply mark it with the date on which you next want to see it and file it, with other similar items, in date order. Then forget it. Waste no more time even thinking about it. You do not have to, because every day you, or your secretary, can check the file and take out anything marked with that day's date. At which point you can either act or, occasionally, give something another date and move it forward.

A couple of provisos must be borne in mind. First, you may want to limit the total quantity of items as something will happen occasionally that means you need to take action earlier than you thought, and you will need to retrieve an item from the file and action it ahead of the date you originally set. Second, you may want to link it to a diary note, especially if you have no secretary. This is a simple, easy to set up, common-sense idea that works for many people.

10.AIM AT INFLUENCING PARTICULAR RESULT AREAS

Everything you do in time management terms is designed to effect efficiency, effectiveness, and productivity; to enable you to do more and to do everything better than would otherwise be the case, so as to achieve the results your job demands. But there are advantages to be gained en route to these ends, and these are useful in their own right.

Considering and keeping specific advantages in mind can help you adopt some of the methodology necessary to an organized way of working and make the whole process easier. Such advantages include:

- Having a clear plan, knowing and having an overview of what must be done—the first step to successfully completing the tasks on your list. Such clarity will make adequate preparation more likely and this can reflect directly on achievement.

- Having a clear link between things to do and overall objectives, which is a sound recipe for keeping on track.
- Being better organized (e.g., not wasting time looking for things).
- Your memory coping better with what you actually need to remember (the systems take care of some of this for you, and it is not necessary to keep everything in your head).
- Being better able to identify and concentrate on the essentials.
- Wasting less energy on irrelevancies.
- Making better decisions about how things should be done (and better business decisions generally).
- Better coordination of tasks (progressing certain things in parallel saves time).
- Having a greater ability to cope with or remove distractions and interruptions.
- Cultivating the habit of greater self-discipline about time matters, which makes consistency of action progressively easier.
- A greater ability to cope with the unexpected and emergency elements of any job.

Any of these are useful, but some may be more useful to you than others, at least at a particular moment.

It may be useful to look for the particular advantage you want: wasting less energy on irrelevancies or, more specifically, attending fewer meetings, for example. Or you may wish to adopt methods that suit you precisely. This is not to say that all those listed above do not have a good general effect on productivity. They do. Focusing what you do carefully will enable you to achieve more, and get greater satisfaction from the results you do achieve.

– Additionally, you may have more time to develop what you do and how you do it, and motivate yourself, all of which can potentially improve things still further. All this may also remove some of the things that create the feeling that a job is "hard work." "Working hard" is nearly always a prerequisite of success, but you do not want tasks to constantly be like trying to nail jam to the wall when a little organization will ensure they go smoothly.

11. USE ABSTRACTS

We live in an information age. But keeping in touch and up to date can be a chore. No one needs reminding of the amount of reading there is to do in most jobs. For some it is very important to keep up to date with the technical area their job involves; for others management processes themselves are worth regular study. In both cases the first task is to decide which, from the plethora of published information, should command your attention. This first selection exercise can be time-consuming of itself before you actually study anything individually.

But help is at hand. In most fields it is possible to subscribe to what are called abstract services. These are not expensive, and from them you receive a regular list of what has been published on a given subject. Such a list does not just contain the titles of articles or papers, but details of the authors, and, most important, synopses of the content. It is this latter information that lets you select with reasonable accuracy those items you judge you want to look at in more detail.

If the thought of this facility appeals to you, then you may want to check what services are available that are relevant to you and your job. Typically they will come from libraries, colleges, trade associations and professional bodies (e.g., management institutes), business schools, and the like. If you find something that offers a service that appears to suit you, then it is perhaps worth taking out a trial subscription to see whether it does save you time. If you find it does, and if it also helps you find information you might otherwise miss, it can then be economic to continue, in which case you have another continuing time saver on your side.

Many abstract services are available online these days and perhaps the first place to check is suitable websites.

12. RECRUIT A GOOD ASSISTANT

There is an old story told of a secretary to a very senior executive who was a frequent traveller. Asked by someone if he could see him, she replied that she was sorry but he was in Hong Kong. "Abroad again," the visitor replied. "He's always overseas. Tell me, who does all his work while he's away?" She looked him straight in the eye and answered without hesitation: "The same person who does it when he's here." Some secretaries perhaps have such authority, but while the secretary is not a panacea, a good one can certainly help.

In the modern workplace secretaries are less common than was once the case. But for those who have one, a good secretary cannot only be the recipient of some of your delegation; they can also act as a regular prompt to good time management and take a genuinely active role in organizing you, or your whole department.

So, what makes the right secretary/PA?

— The characteristics of the ideal secretary are legion. As well as typing, and sometimes shorthand, skills, she must be familiar with an increasing array of office technology. In addition, it helps if she is patient, is gifted with second sight, and has two

> pairs of hands. But what of time management? Whether she has a natural or acquired organizational ability is difficult to assess at an interview, as is whether she really cares about such things. If, however, you can make such an assessment, and are able to appoint a candidate who has characteristics of this sort, then you will have a real asset on board in your battle to win the time war.

When recruiting, ask any questions you can think of that will give you information in this area, particularly about past experience in managing the diary, appointments, and projects of those she has worked for previously. This is also something to check in taking up references (always a wise precaution).

There are two other important characteristics that you should seek. First, that she will work your way. This is essential as there may be existing procedures and systems, as well as management style, that you need her to fit in with; on the other hand, always be ready to learn from her. There is no monopoly on good ideas, the only criterion being that the ideas are useful. Second, that she has sufficient "weight" or clout; that is, she must be able to stand up for you with colleagues and others, to say "no" on your behalf, and to make requests on your behalf—and make them stick.

Achieve this and your attempts to control your time will have a permanent ally: one who will work with you to achieve what you want and who will, at best and with experience, take an active role in the process. One final point—if you share a secretary or assistant, this does not negate what is said here, though achieving an operational consensus may take a moment and some sensible collaboration.

13. COMMUNICATE WITH YOUR SECRETARY

It is not much use having a good secretary (or assistant), one who is sympathetic to time management, and then not communicating with her.

Communicate: there may seem never to be time for this, but if you do find the time for it, then it will help you save much more time than this communication takes. Many executives start the day with a meeting with their secretary, perhaps when the mail arrives in the morning. You must decide what suits you best and also work out a way of keeping in touch and up to date with her if you spend much time out of the office, though modern communications make this easier than once was the case.

Your secretary must know how you work and know what you have on the go at any particular time. And she should, if possible, share your view of priorities, knowing what you are prepared to be interrupted for, which things and people rate most time and attention, and which tasks come first. Once she has some experience, more may well be possible. She can take the initiative on things, accompany you to certain meetings, and ultimately run whole areas of your office life in a way that increases your utilization of time dramatically. Find areas of real responsibility, let her look after them and make the decisions affecting them, and it can pay dividends.

Communication is the one prerequisite for creating a good working relationship. If lack of communication causes problems—a string of time-wasting meetings in your diary as you come back from a trip, say—then consider the fault yours. Communicate clearly and regularly, and remember that includes listening.

14. BE BRIEF

Clearly, brevity in communications saves everybody

time; for you in writing something, for the recipient in reading it.

The idea here is simple: Be brief. Do not succumb to verbal diarrhea and keep things simple. Easy?

The pressures of the modern workplace and the almost universal use of email have forced into better practice with regard to brevity. But there is a caveat. However brief, messages must be clear. If brief, your written communication may be less time-consuming to create, but any misunderstandings it may give rise to will just jack up the time involved as things are sorted out. So, choosing words carefully, you need to be succinct and precise and, of course, clear.

15. A CLEAR DIARY

However well organized you may be or get to be, you cannot hope to keep all the details of what you will do when in your head.

A good, clear diary system is a must. Many formal systems combine the conventional diary with their sophisticated version of the "to do" list. One thing that certainly works well, and which a loose-leaf system allows, is to have at one opening of a binder a complete picture of your day, showing both appointments and things to do. Thus you might allocate a couple of hours to write a report.

What form it takes is a matter of choice; though bear in mind the concept of a "master diary": one place needs to have the definitive record if you are to avoid coming into the office with an appointment to list and finding that someone has double-booked you.

Small things have an effect on efficiency. The diary should:

- Show full details, certainly full enough to be clear. An entry that reads 'R.B. Lunch' tells you little—where is it, at what time is it, can you be contacted while you are out, how long will it last, and, not least, are you even going to remember in three weeks' time to whom R.B. refers? If you want a real horror story, I know of a case where all it said in someone's diary was the name of a town, with two days ruled out. He was away, presumably staying at a hotel, and had only told his family to contact him via his office. When one of his children was involved in an accident, it took two days before the message reached him. His diary was a copybook example of clarity thereafter.
- Show how long is set aside for things.
- Schedule all of your working time rather than just appointments, perhaps the most important and useful difference between just an appointments diary and a time management system. The two additions are tasks, actually setting aside time to work on a specific project, and thinking time so that creative work is not carried out, as so often happens, only in gaps that are left between appointments. If this is done—leaving space for the unexpected or reactive part of the work, whatever proportion that is—and linked to the concept of a rolling plan, you will stay more organized and be able to judge much better how things are progressing, whether deadlines will be met and tasks completed.
- Be completed in pencil so that alterations can be made without creating an illegible mess.

Two final points. First, the diary is a vital tool, to be guarded and treated with respect. A conventional diary is also therefore a good place to keep other key information, telephone numbers, and other data you need at your fingertips, provided you do not overburden it so that it becomes too thick and unmanageable. Second, the computer, and a variety of electronic personal organizers, are taking over some of these activities. Often this works well. Being able to set up a meeting with six colleagues, some in different cities, at the touch of a button on a networked system may well save time.

For many people a personal diary or planner, in the old sense of something that works anywhere there is a pencil, will always be a part of what helps them work effectively. Certainly the thinking that needs to be applied to diary organization is the same however the information involved may be recorded.

16. WHAT KIND OF SYSTEM?

Many books on the subject of time management are closely linked to some specific proprietary time management system, consisting of diaries, files, binders, and in some cases more besides. Some even claim that the only route to time efficiency lies with the particular system they recommend. Now this may be fine if the system suits you, but I would suggest caution in taking up any particular system.

A better way is perhaps to work out what you need first: what kind of diary, how much space for notes, how many sections to fit the way your tasks are grouped, what permanent filing. Then, when you have thought through what you need and worked that way for a while (a process that will almost certainly have you making a few changes in the light of how things actually work), you can check out the systems and see whether any of them formalise what you want to do and, as they can be expensive, get one knowing that the investment is worth while.

The world is full of people who organize themselves perfectly well with no more than a diary, a notebook, or a file. This combines a neat system with the flexibility to put in exactly what you need, and that is what is most important. After all, it must reflect your plan and it is your time that you want to organize. Such can be desk or pocket sized.

17. TRUST THE COMPUTER

It has become one of the great myths of the IT age that computers will transform office work, and make everything fast and efficient to action. But like other great promises—*Our cheque is in the post*—it is not entirely to be trusted. Now I have nothing against computers and there are things that one cannot now imagine working any other way. And yet . . . there are questions, certainly as far as efficiency and time utilization are concerned, at desk level for the individual executive. There are examples of things now available that manifestly (mostly!) work well. Such include: databases, graphics programs, email, and desktop publishing—all have advantages over equivalents that do not involve computers.

Yet there are systems that for all their cleverness do not fit their role so well. Think of some of the systems you may be frustrated by as a customer, in the bank, with an insurance company, or at a hotel. Take a hotel account as an example. They are, one presumes, efficient for the hotel but many are very difficult for the guest to fathom without a degree in abbreviations. It is customer service that has suffered in this case.

Think carefully before you agree to computerise something assuming doing so "must make it better."

There is another side to computers: you (well, many of us) need expert help to set up many systems (and in some cases to operate them), there is a high capital cost (though this is coming down), and they are all too readily used as an excuse for not doing things.

18. CANCELLATION AS A TIME SAVER

This is a brief point, and links to the topic of meetings, which crops up in more than one section. There is an issue here that can waste large amounts of time. It is surprising and curious how meetings that are scheduled for a good reason still run even when not only has the good reason gone but everyone knows it has gone. It is difficult to understand. Perhaps someone thinks it is too late to cancel, or they think that it will still be useful as minor matters can be dealt with "as the people are coming together anyway."

Usually the thinking above is wrong. It is better to cancel the meeting, or postpone it if the main reason for it has not gone away forever.

This principle is especially true of regular series of meetings. The example of ten meetings being held through a year is the kind of thing where it is often better to schedule ten knowing you are in fact likely only to need eight or nine. The disruption of one dropped is very much less than pulling an extra one together at short notice, and this should become the habit. Never go ahead just because it is "the regular meeting" or you will waste time.

There is even a case for refusing to use words such as weekly or monthly in the title of a meeting; it can end up prompting meetings that prove useless.

19. MOTIVATE YOUR PEOPLE

Motivation is a powerful force. If you are a manager, then it makes people perform better and that saves time.

Simply stated—the idea is to motivate people. If the team you manage are well motivated, then they will perform better, with less input from you; it is a formula that saves the manager time and makes for an all-round more productive team. The problem is that this does not just happen. It takes some time. Without doing so, however, you will not get the best from people, and that means some time will be wasted. Again, the equation of time here makes sense: the net effect should be a saving.

Motivation has been described as a climate and this is not a bad analogy. Just like the climate or the temperature in a room, it is affected by many different things, and the effect can be for good or ill. There is sadly no magic formula for guaranteeing that motivation will be, and will stay, high. You have to look at the motivational implications of things such as the administration and systems with which people work, the way they relate to colleagues and you as supervisor, their feeling of security in the sense of knowing what they have to do and being part of a good team. All these can pull motivation down if they are organized badly or unsympathetically.

Similarly, there are many influences that boost people's motivation such as the enjoyment of the work and, more particularly, a sense of satisfaction and achievement in doing it and doing it well. All these and more are important—and it is a subject worth some study if you manage others.

The details of what motivates people are beyond the brief here, but one thing is worth a mention: small things matter. People do not just like to achieve, they like recognition of that to be shown. Yet most people who are busy cannot, in all honesty, put their hands on their hearts and say that they always remember the little things as much as they should. Think about it yourself.

Have you said "thank you" or "well done" often enough lately? It matters, people notice and they expect it. You have time for that—and it will save you time.

Remember, motivation is essentially long term. It's an ongoing process to change attitudes and you should not expect instant results; rather you should see a variety of actions as creating over time a productive team that will then work effectively in all the ways that make your time go further.

20. THINKING AHEAD

This might appropriately be called the opposite of the "if only . . ." school of ineffective time management. Too often managers find themselves in a crisis that would be all too easily resolved if they could wind the clocks back.

If you can acquire the habit of thinking ahead and take a systematic view of things, then you are that much more likely to see when a start really needs to be made on something. If things are left late or ill thought out, then time is used up in a hasty attempt to sort things out at short notice. This tends to make any task more difficult and is compounded by whatever day-to-day responsibilities are current at the time.

21. SEE THE BROAD PICTURE

Not everyone works solely on a day-to-day basis. Many people have to operate in a way that involves keeping in mind a span of time that may be weeks, months, or even years in extent. Here, a particular approach can enhance the practicality of a diary.

Using a planner element within a diary is very useful. Anyone who needs to take an overview of a period and see how various different things relate one to another is likely to find it invaluable.

The mental process of seeing a span of time, rather than thumbing through pages, is really helpful in managing any kind of project. Care here can prevent missed deadlines and that can save more than time.

Be careful of taking time in duplication. For instance, some people enter everything in three places: a diary, a planning chart, and a separate wall planner. Additional recording may be necessary too, such as a separate chart to plan and monitor people's holidays. If you want to use a planning chart as your sole diary device, why not do so? The key is to keep a handle on the whole of your schedule no matter what length of time this encompasses.

22. AVOIDING A COMMON CONFUSION

Most people are in agreement about their work situation. In a word, you are busy. There are so many things to do and insufficient time in which to do them all. Furthermore, the picture changes as you watch. Just as you get one thing done and dusted, others join the queue. The mail arrives, you open your email, someone comes up to your desk and asks a favour, the boss says, "This is urgent" . . .

The principle here is trite, a cliché, but it is also a truism. The right approach here is itself a major contributor to personal productivity. It is simply that you should: Never confuse activity with achievement.

Recognizing that there is a difference between what is urgent and what is important must become a reflex for the effective time manager. Diversions, distractions, and peripheral activity of all sorts must be recognized and kept in their place.

This must be a permanent state of mind; in effect it is one of the guiding principles that help ensure a productive approach. Not only must the positive aspect of this be kept in mind; so must the tendency to rationalise the wrong things for the wrong reason, categorizing something as important when it is not.

Priorities, dealt with elsewhere, must be just that—and the measure of what is a priority must always include the measure: does this link to planned results?

23. "EVERYBODY'S GONE SURFING, SURFING . . ."

Here's something that has become a real hazard in recent years and must waste uncounted hours in offices around the world. What's that? The internet: or, more specifically, non-work-related surfing.

The idea is simple: don't engage in non-work-related surfing.

The worst time-waster in this area is probably social websites such as Facebook. Time very quickly disappears as you dip "just once more" into a chat site. And if you doubt the danger and want another thought that might reinforce the truth, it is reckoned that a high percentage of all the hits on pornographic sites are made between 9 a.m. and 5 p.m. when presumably most computer users are at work!

24. TELEPHONE EFFICIENCY

If you make any number of telephone calls as part of your job, it can seem unbelievable how much time is wasted dialing, redialing, and holding on the telephone. Much of this time is these days spent listening to a unique and repetitive form of music that has been known to send even the sanest into unreasonable states, and working your way through endless "press this option" sequences. The simplest way of avoiding all this is to get your secretary to obtain calls for you, but her time is valuable too and, besides, fewer and fewer people have one.

What does make a real difference is a modern telephone. This is a form of new technology I really warm to, not so complicated that it puts you off and with specific features that are real time savers. For example:

- If you have the ability to store all the common numbers you use, this will save you having to dial them—a couple of digits and the phone does the rest.
- Many will also redial (for example, if the chosen number is busy first time) and some will go on and on dialing automatically until they get through.
- A loudspeaker means that if you have to hold on (listening to the music) then your hands are free and work can continue.

The features of telephones expand with the march of time, and many save time. In addition, you can sometimes reduce the time taken up by the endless options through which it is necessary to run the gauntlet before you get through to who you want. Keep a note of the option numbers for organizations you call regularly; you can often press a number as soon as a list starts rather than waiting until the number you want is given.

25. A LITTLE HELP FROM SOME "SPECIAL" FRIENDS

One option is to use, albeit at a cost, one of the concierge services that have sprung up in recent years. What do they do? Well, one of the best known is Quintessentially, which describes itself as the world's leading luxury lifestyle group focused on providing its members with the best things in life. I phoned their offices and my friend told me, "With thousands of suppliers across the globe, Quintessentially offers an unrivalled worldwide network and is able to offer discounts and added value with only the very best of products and services.

Since its launch in 2000, Quintessentially has added a portfolio of 14 sister businesses encompassing property, events, wine, art consultancy, and even a modelling agency. They have 44 offices in a host of major cities worldwide including destinations as diverse as Buenos Aires, Cape Town, Dubai, Los Angeles, Moscow, Shanghai, and Sydney and aim to save their members time, hassle, and money.

Such services cost, of course, and may thus be only for those at a senior level or who can persuade their company to budget for it. Nevertheless they deserve a mention here. The time such services can save is considerable and the good operations are well set up. Even when travelling, you can make one phone call in the middle of the night (from a different time zone), arrange to be picked up at the airport, get the dishwasher at home fixed before you get back, and set up a meeting with your bank to explain just why you have been spending so extensively in some obscure foreign currency. Quintessentially has had some exceptional, even oddball, successes: ranging from organizing a visit to the North Pole to see the Northern Lights to having a Premier League soccer player attend the birthday of one member's twin sons for a kick-about.

26. GIVE YOURSELF SOME TIME RULES

When things get left, as they can easily do, then it can cause problems, and those problems can waste more time. Something is late. Someone chases. You respond (with excuses?). Moving into firefighting mode, you clear a gap, maybe affecting other matters, and then the omission is made good.

There is a whole category of things where a simple rule will avoid them being overlooked and causing the sequence of events give yourself an "action now" time rule that prompts to get something out of the way and helps make doing so a habit.

You can choose the time extent. You might select two minutes. If something appears needing action and you reckon it can be done in a couple of minutes—do it at once and get it out of the way.

The time needs to fit your work and activity. For some people it might be two minutes, or ten or something in between, but the assessment you make and how you act because of it can keep what may be a significant percentage of your tasks on the move in a way that prevents them being likely to get delayed or cause problems.

This is an example of a wholly self-imposed discipline, but one that can work well and add to your time management effectiveness just a little more.

27. DON'T WRITE

Paper clogs up most workplaces—is all your paperwork really necessary? Much of it will be, but some paperwork can be eliminated.

Resolve always to pause for a second before you write and ask yourself whether what you are about to do is really necessary.

The key alternative to written communication is the telephone; it is usually much quicker to lift the telephone than to write something, and, as not everything needs a written record, this is one of the surest ways of reducing paperwork.

It is also worth making a note here about the now ubiquitous email, also an alternative to more formal communication. It is not so much the sense of urgency this bestows on things that interests in this context: it is the style. It seems to be that an altogether less formal style has developed for the email. It is one that is perfectly acceptable internally around a big organization with a number of offices, and with people in other organizations, as a quick form of communication where brevity is of the essence. A small point here: email files must be well managed and some must be printed out.

Two other points are worth a mention. The first is unnecessary copies. Second, see if something can be standardized. There may be a number of routine communications that can be retained as standard documents— for example, either whole letters or contracts or separate paragraphs that can be used to put together something suitable. Here technology really does save time. But there is one very important caveat here: never, never use standard material if it is inappropriate. In the sales area, for example, I come across many letters and proposals that shout "standard" when they should be seen as an individual response to the individual customer who receives them. Further, any standard material should be double-checked to ensure that it is well written. Otherwise, by definition, something poor or, at worst, damaging may be sent out hundreds of times a month. It can certainly save time but should not do so at the cost of an unacceptable reduction in quality.

28. AVOID PURPOSELESS MEETINGS

When did you last lose patience in a meeting? Meetings are held every day without real—or clear—objectives, and take longer and become muddled as a result. And "objectives" does not mean meeting to:

- Start the planning process.
- Discuss cost savings.
- Review training needs.
- Streamline administration.

— Explore time saving measures.

All meetings should have clear objectives and these should be specific. So saying you will discuss how you might save 10 per cent on the advertising budget over the next six months is clear. Better still if that is a figure picked as achievable and it is something currently necessary (despite the effects it might have).

So a specific statement of objectives—which should be in writing in many cases and circulated to all those due to participate—will have a number of effects:

- People will be clear why the meeting is being held.
- They will be better able, and perhaps more inclined, to prepare.
- Discussion will be easier to control, as people will focus more on the topic and the meeting will be more likely to achieve the desired result and to do so in less time than would be the case with a vague description.

So, if you ever go to meetings where the objectives do not seem to be clear, ask what they are. Others may well agree that they are not clear, and a few minutes spent early in the meeting clarifying this may be time well spent rather than launching into discussion and finding that the meeting grinds to a halt in confusion half an hour later. Better still, ask before you attend. A clear objective is a real necessity; no meeting without this is likely to conclude its business either promptly or satisfactorily.

29. HANDLING TELEPHONE INTERRUPTIONS

The telephone has an insistency that is not easily ignored. Whatever your work pattern, no doubt sometimes you want to be immediately accessible, and on other occasions a task will be completed quicker if you are uninterrupted. Maybe you can get a secretary or assistant to act as a buffer taking calls in the first instance. Clear briefing can rapidly establish those callers you will pause for, those whom to tell you will call back, and those to forget. This option may not be available, but if you take the call yourself you are at a considerable advantage compared with facing the head round your office door: the caller cannot see you.

You must resolve to *decide* whether to take calls or not. Some are clearly so important that they override other considerations—in other cases you need to reduce the interruptions. There are certainly people who do not regard saying they are busy, in a meeting, just leaving the office, or similar statements as too much of a white lie if it fends off an unwanted interruption.

In all circumstances, people know and understand, from their own experience, that the phone can be intrusive and tend to be more understanding of your not necessarily welcoming a call at a particular moment. So be firm and you will save time.

All matters of handling these kinds of people interruptions require the normal people-handling skills: tact, diplomacy, but also suitable assertiveness. These need to be deployed in the right mix and to the appropriate degree. If you are seen as insensitive and assertive to the point of rudeness, this may well be destructive of relationships. But if you effectively lie down and ask to be walked on, then it should be no surprise when you are treated like a doormat.

Even more important is the resolve and tenacity that you put into establishing approaches here. Some people—who doubtless work at it—are conspicuously more successful than others at avoiding interruptions. Precedents are easily set, for good or ill. There is a great deal to be gained by getting things right in this area and that includes ensuring you are seen in the right kind of way.

30. KEEP PAPERS SAFE AND TIDY

It is a small point perhaps, but you can waste some considerable time hunting for papers and re-collating papers that have got out of order in this sort of way.

Paper clips are not the best way to keep papers tidy. Beware—they do tend to trap other items and catch you unawares. So save time by banning them and seek another way.

To help ensure that your papers are kept tidy, do not keep too much together, and worry in particular about files and papers that travel about with you both around and out of the office. Staple them, punch them, or bind them rather than use paper clips, and experiment with whatever sort offiles—and there are many different styles—suit you. I favour the sort that have a small top and bottom flap to hold things all round and elastic bands that snap across the corners.

The more things you have to work on in parallel the more your current papers need organizing neatly. If you only get one file out at a time and work on that until it is neatly replaced by something else, then it is less of a problem, but realistically you probably need more around you. If you are paid to keep many balls in the air at once, then this is vital. Time management is, in this respect, similar to juggling. If there are a lot of balls in the air and one is dropped, more tend to follow. The more you have on the go, the greater the disruption and waste of time if something becomes disorganized. Always keep papers physically under control.

31. DO NOT PUT IT IN WRITING

While he had lavished care and attention—and thus

time—on what was a 20-page report, he was unprepared for this and his spur-of-the-moment presentation was not as fluent as he would have wished. Its writer was naturally aggrieved and resented the incident—with some cause perhaps.

Certainly management ought to consider the consequences of its action, decisions, and requests to others in time terms. What avoids something taking up time for you may land someone else with a great deal of extra work. If you are a manager, your responsibility for good time utilization covers the team. It is little good being productive yourself if everyone else is tied up with all sorts of unnecessary tasks and paperwork. Jobs need to be done, action taken, consideration given, and in many cases written instructions, guidelines, or confirmation are not simply necessary: they are vital. But on other occasions that may well not be the case. This kind of thing can often happen. Time may be wasted unless the instigator of such action thinks first and only specifies whatever action is really necessary.

Where does the responsibility for such occurrences lie? It is easy to blame management, but those in receipt of such requests should not be afraid to ask, and check whether such tasks are really necessary. Whichever category of person you are in, and it may well be both, give it a thought.

Of course, there are other considerations. If you just say, "Shan't" next time the managing director asks for a report, do not come crying to me if you are read the riot act.

32. A MAGIC WORD

Everyone has to accept that they cannot do everything. This must probably be taken literally because there may be an almost infinite amount to do, particularly in any job that has some kind of inherent innovative or creative nature to it. Many people could just go on listing more and more things to do, not all equally important, but deserving of a place on their "to do" list nevertheless. Even if your job is not like this, you certainly have to accept that you are not going to do everything at the time you want.

For reasons of workload and priorities, you are going to have to say "no" to some things. Regularly, and with many people, you need to resolve to think before you agree, and to turn down involvements in some things even though they would be attractive to you. Agreeing to things you should turn down will lead you away from priorities; saying "no" is a fundamental time saver. It was well put by Charles Spurgeon: *Learn to say no; it will be more use to you than to be able to read Latin.*

For instance you may have to turn down:

- *Colleagues*: What is involved here can vary, and if there is a network of favours, with everyone helping everyone else, you do not want to let it get out of hand either way. Turn down too much and you end up losing time because people are reluctant to help you. Do everything unquestioningly and you may be seen as a soft touch and will end up doing more than your share. So balance is the keynote here. Timing is important too; you do not have to do everything you agree to instantly.
- *Subordinates*: Here they cannot tell you to do things, and, though they need support, this must not get out of hand—choose how long you spend with them and ensure the time spent is worth while.
- *Your boss*: Working with a boss who does not have enough to do, or who expects everything to be done instantly just because they are in charge, can play havoc with the best intentions of time

management. You may need to regard it as your mission to educate them and have to conduct a campaign of persuasion and negotiation to keep any unreasonable load down.

33. THE PRODUCTIVE BREATHER

Take a break: an occasional break does not reduce your productivity; it actually helps it. You return to your desk with your head clearer; you feel refreshed and revived by stretching your limbs and can get back to the task in hand with renewed fervour.

This is particularly true of seemingly intractable tasks. Sometimes you can sit and puzzle about things for a long time and appear to get nowhere. After a break it suddenly becomes clear— or at least clearer— and time is saved as a result. Sometimes a break may be as simple as standing up and stretching, or making a cup of tea. Or it may be that something that takes a bit longer is better—you go to lunch even though you originally planned to do that an hour later, or you go for a walk. Once I shared an office with someone who did this—the office was opposite a park and he had a particular circuit that took about ten minutes and provided useful thinking time, perhaps being applied to something else apart from the job from which he had paused. This made a real break, yet was still productive.

Recognize that a break is often much more productive than struggling on with a job when concentration is not adequate. Alternatively, switch tasks for a moment, rather than stop work, in order to ring the changes.

34. A COSMIC DANGER

In most offices there are corporate equivalents of this phenomenon, "black hole jobs" that suck in all the time you can think of and a bit more.

Watch out for such jobs and beware—just like real black holes, if you get too near there is no going back and an involvement means all your other plans have to be put on hold. What kind of jobs warrant this description? They are usually projects involving a number of different tasks. They are often contentious, may involve an impossibility of pleasing everyone and can be ruinous of reputations, as well as taking up a quite disproportionate amount of time. They include a range of things from arranging the organization's twentieth anniversary party and celebrations to planning the move to new offices. Such things have to be done, but they often call for "volunteers." This can mean the managing director suggests it, in public, in a way that makes refusal risky: *It is only a suggestion, of course, but do bear in mind who's making it.* At this point others heave sighs of relief and resolve not to get involved even in a tiny support role.

You will know, if you have any wits at all, the kind of tasks in your office that have these characteristics and should, if you value your ability to keep on top of your other tasks, plan to be well away whenever there is a danger of you getting lumbered with one. Do not say you have not been warned.

35. TIME TO STAY PUT

Thousands of journeys must be undertaken every day that are not really necessary. All over the world taxis, cars, trains, and planes are taking people to places to see other people where face-to-face contact is not strictly required. The attendant cost and time cannot even be guessed at.

Where some form of personal contact is necessary, always consider the alternatives, and resist the reflex that has you rushing away; even a trip from one side of a city to another is time-consuming.

Practice the following:

- *Have people come to you:* this may be possible, you may only have to suggest it or it may even be worth footing the bill, providing an overnight hotel stay; this will cost no more than you travelling in the reverse direction, and saves you time.
- *Send someone else:* yes, even to that attractively located conference—delegate.
- *Telephone:* some things really can be dealt with pretty simply and you do not need to be face to face, or an initial telephone contact gets things started with a visit coming later if necessary.
- Write or email.
- *Use technology:* for those who are able to afford it, modern telecommunications offers a range of increasingly sophisticated possibilities, including telephone and videoconferencing where you can be linked electronically to a group of people all able to converse and even see each other at the same time, regardless of location.

You do not have to be very numerate to work out how much time could be saved over a year if you cut out even a small proportion of your journeys, one a month, one a week—the hours saved quickly mount up. So before buying a ticket, think for a moment. Of course some things can genuinely only be dealt with face to face and some journeys are essential—but not all.

36. WHEN BEING REGULAR IS A PROBLEM

Here is something that occurs in many organizations. There are monthly, weekly, even daily meetings that are held on that particular frequency for no better reason than that they have become a habit. Sometimes, of course, these are necessary, but on other occasions there is nothing, or nothing very much, to discuss and the meeting may then be padded out to make it worth while.

This practice can lead so easily to time being wasted that it is a good idea to avoid anything having the name "monthly so and so meeting"; it makes it just too easy to keep them going—needed or not.

If a meeting is to be held a number of times through the year, consider not just the frequency, but specifically the number and placement of such meetings. For example, maybe you do not need 12 monthly meetings but ten instead, and at some times of the year you need them closer together, while at others you can have longer gaps between them. This kind of scheduling will almost always save time.

It is also good practice to schedule a number of meetings well ahead. So, for the situation referred to above, you would set ten dates for the year ahead, adding a new tenth date at each meeting to keep the future arrangement the same. Everyone knows the problem of getting a group of busy people together at short notice, so this will always work well, particularly if the people involved are disciplined about their diaries and do not allow themselves to be double-booked. Certain meetings are clearly priority occasions and should be regarded as such, remembering that any change disrupts a number of people and thus wastes a disproportionate amount of time.

In this way meetings will be perceived as reflecting their role, rather than any mechanistic formula of, for example, "meeting once a month."

37. TIME TO GET NOTICED

Not everything needs to employ high-tech communication or be passed on instantly; for certain kinds of information old-fashioned methods are still best.

Use a bulletin board. A strategically placed notice-board can keep people up to speed on a number of things and creates a place where information can linger for a while. It is useful, for example, in giving news of someone's promotion an airing that extends the motivational impact of such an announcement.

If your office, or company or department, does not have a bulletin board, get one soon, and then make it clear to people that certain things will not be circulated widely. A brief notice posted once can save time and it quickly becomes a habit for people to look—worth a try!

38. MOST TIME-SAVING OBJECT IN YOUR OFFICE

All sorts of things cross your desk: magazines, direct mail, items marked "To read and circulate" and "For information," copies of things that are of no real relevance to you, and minutes of meetings that you wish had never taken place. Much of this pauses for far too long, creating heaps and extra filing trays on your desk and bundles in your briefcase. It is better to deal with things early rather than later. When they have mounted up, they are always going to be more difficult to get through, and an immediate decision will keep the volume down.

What is the most time saving object in your office? The WPB. The idea here involves the simple premise of throwing things away. The WPB is, of course, the wastepaper basket. It helps efficiency and time if your desk and office are tidy, if what you need is neatly and accessibly placed—a place for everything and everything in its place—but not if such good order is submerged under sheer quantity of paper, most of it of a "just in case" nature. Clear the clutter and throw unnecessary things away.

If you are on a circulation list and do not want to look at something today, then add your name further down the list and pass it on; it will get back to you later when you may be less busy.

At least check things like a trade magazine at once; maybe you can tear out an article or two and throw the rest away.

Consider very carefully whether the vast plethora of things that "might be useful" is, in fact, ever likely to be, and either file them or throw them away—regularly.

All such thinking and action help, but most people are conservative and somehow reluctant to throw things away. Unless you are very untypical, there will be things on and around your desk right now that could be thrown out. Have a look, and, as you look, do some throwing. Make a full WPB a target for the end of the day. Imagine it has a scale running down the inside to show how full it is. Such a scale could almost be graduated, not in volume, but in minutes saved.

39. THE CONFLICT/TIME EQUATION

Now listen, pay attention. It is no good just sitting there lazily scanning the pages, you have to read this properly and . . . Not a good start. Sometimes an approach that is designed to get straight to the point and therefore not waste time has the reverse effect: it rubs people up the wrong way. This ends up producing misunderstanding, dissent, or argument. All of which take time to resolve and the original intention goes out the window. Conflict is not, in fact, entirely bad. It can act as a catalyst to debate, it can help promote creativity and serve to drive for the results necessary in business. But there is a real difference between this and allowing unnecessary conflict to disrupt the smooth running of things and your time being affected along with it.

The wrong decisions should be made for the sake of a quiet life, but in a number of areas it is a good idea for conflict to be avoided; if unnecessary conflict is absent, then time is surely saved.

An approach designed to minimize conflict can take many forms, for example:

- In communications: it may be necessary to persuade rather than cajole, and time taken to do so successfully may pay dividends.
- Office politics can become intrusive and time-consuming; though ignoring it is dangerous in other ways, it must be kept in its place.
- Personalities can become more important than issues; commercial reason must dictate most of what directs an organization, and untangling personality factors once they have got out of hand takes time.
- Sectional interests also have to be watched.

Operationally, the first step is for consideration of what will be decided, with any discussions, meetings, and everything to do with the process to be kept primarily on a practical basis. If conflict—for instance, about personal issues— is avoided, then the time taken to sort something out will almost certainly be less.

40. TOO MANY HEAD CHEFS

With the budgetary pressure on many organizations these days, it is not uncommon for staffing levels to be under pressure too, and one symptom of this may be that organization structure is made to accommodate multiple reporting relationships.

Avoid anyone in any way having two bosses; it is never ideal. There are likely to be clashes in priorities. Unless there is a clear hierarchy—for instance, with two people sharing a secretary/ assistant—there will be problems: whose work gets done first? It could be that an arrangement is fine most of the time, but when it causes problems it tends to cause awkward ones and the likelihood is that something will end up being late. The other example above may pose much more radical clashes: maybe a proposed new programme to be used in the computer department suits one of its masters and not the other. Buying two versions might double an already significant cost. Who wins?

The one certainty with any situation of this kind is that sorting out the overlaps takes time, actual productivity is reduced, and time is taken up on activity only made necessary by the way things are organized.

Multi-boss reporting is not usually a good idea. It affects the people involved, and may regularly put them in awkward positions between the two parties.

Multi-boss reporting also affects other management issues: who appraises the person, who sets their salary, who is actually the overall supervisor? All such things are made more difficult.

So there are a number of good reasons to avoid this situation, and time management that achieves suitable productivity is a key one.

41. AN IDEA THAT GENERATES IDEAS

You have all sorts of things to do and all sorts of different kinds of things too—all varying in importance, of course. It is usually true to say that the higher up the hierarchy of an organization you go, the more time you are expected to spend thinking, planning, and decision-making and the less doing other things. It is also often true that any thinking, the planning and idea generation that goes into a job, is usually one of the most important things to be done in that job.

There is a good training movie on aspects of time management. At the end of the movie the main character, a manager who has come to grips with managing his time better, is sitting in his office. A colleague comes into the outer office and begins to walk past the secretary to see him. She stops him, says her manager is busy, and suggests he makes an appointment to see him later. He looks past her at the manager sitting in his office and says: *But he's not doing anything!* Immediately the secretary replies: *He's thinking; now do you want to see him this afternoon or . . .* This incident makes a good point.

What is the most difficult kind of time to keep clear and have sufficient of? Time to think—and think creatively—always ranks high. The moral is clear: one of the most important things your time management practices have to do is to make room for the thinking and creative time your job needs.

Consider any analysis of your time you have done, or better still your time log if you have done one, and see how creative activities show up. If they are not getting the time they need and deserve or are being squeezed out by other pressures and what seems more obviously urgent, then you need to actively seek a better balance.

Make sure that you set your sights on sufficient thinking time— perhaps above all—and that the action you take to achieve this is not offset by the crises that all too easily beset any organization or department. Without something approaching the ideal in this area, all your objectives may be in jeopardy.

42. REWARD YOURSELF

Because time management is not straightforward—indeed, it requires regular thought—it is easy to take your eyes off the ball and find that your good intentions are not being met.

If you motivate yourself and give yourself some real reasons to make time management tactics work, you will be more successful at it. Give yourself time management incentives. You need something more than just getting to the bottom of your in-tray. In any case, even the most effective person may never do this, and, while achieving more than expected is perhaps reward enough in some ways, what is wanted is something that is linked more specifically to your own success in managing your time.

It thus makes sense to set yourself specific time management goals and to link them to what that will do for you : to give yourself personal satisfaction so that you are very aware that succeeding in what you intend in time terms will make something else possible.

If you can think in this kind of way and give yourself some sort of reward—better still, a number of them—then your focus on what time management can do for you will be maintained.

43. BEST TIME FOR APPOINTMENTS

Appointments—interactions WITH other people—take up a major amount of many executives' time. Many of these occur on a planned basis: they are scheduled appointments.

Recognize that exactly when you program appointments makes a real difference to your productivity and think carefully about their scheduling. Allow sufficient time; one appointment running into another always causes problems. And always schedule a period of time—in other words, a finishing time as well as a start time. It is impossible to do this with 100 percent accuracy, but it helps to aim for what's ideal.

Think about:

- *The potential for interruptions:* an early meeting, before the office switchboard opens, may take less time because there are fewer interruptions.
- *The location:* where it is geographically makes a difference, and a meeting room may be better than your office, especially if you need to clear the decks and move what you are working on just before it starts.
- Timing that makes it inevitable that it continues into lunch or a drink at the end of the day.
- Timing that restricts your ability to schedule other appointments, in the sense that something mid-morning could mean there is not sufficient time to fit in another meeting before it, or after it and before lunch.

And take especial care with gatherings that involve more than one other person. You have to be accommodating here, but do not always consider others' convenience before your own—it is you who will suffer. Record appointments clearly in the diary and consider separately the various aspects of meetings commented on in a number of other sections.

44. ONE THING AT A TIME

The disparate nature of the tasks most people handle makes managing them difficult. You tend to flit from one to another and need different things in place to tackle each.

Another overriding principle of good time management is to batch your tasks. Here again proprietary time management systems all have their own methodology, and it is in some cases over-complicated, certainly for my taste, but of course what works best for you is the only measure. More important than the precise configuration of the system here is the number of categories: three to six are ideal simply because that is manageable. It does not matter too much what you call them:

- Priority.
- Important.
- Action now.
- Obtain more information.
- Reading.

These are just some of the options (and there are those who manage perfectly well with A, B, and C).

The key thing is to match the categories to the way you work, for instance:

- You may need file and may consider other action categories such as telephone, dictate, write, and document, and similar ones that are particular to your business and your role in it such as proposals, quotations, or the names of products, departments, or systems.
- An important area these days is things that demand you go online. If you have a variety of (genuine) tasks that need you to work in this way, time may well be saved by batching them together.
- A manageable number of batches of this sort can, if you wish, link physically to filing trays on your desk or some distinguishing mark on files themselves.

45. AT THE BOTTOM OF THE PILE

The need to recognize priorities pervades all thinking about time management. While it is important to identify and deal with key priorities, an inappropriate reordering can occur for the wrong reasons. Things get sidelined for various reasons; here's one deceptively simple one many people fall foul of (and one to be honest about).

There is a difference between what you find difficult and what you simply do not like. The likely effect of delay and avoidance of tasks is here very similar to that for things found difficult, but the motivation is different, though nonetheless powerful.

There can be numerous reasons for disliking doing something: it involves something else you do not like, maybe for the best motives (perhaps doing something necessitates a visit to a regional office, which will take up a whole day and involve an awkward journey), or, more often, the dislike is minor—it is just a chore, or a chore compared with other things on your "to do" list. This is perhaps the chief reason why administration is so often in arrears. It is boring and there are other things to do and . . . but you doubtless know the feeling.

The only real help here is self-discipline and a conscious effort in planning what you do to make sure that such things do not get left out and that this, in turn does not lead to worse problems. Some flagging system to highlight things on your "hate" list may act as a psychological prompt; experiment here to see if it makes a difference.

If all this seems minor and you disbelieve the impact of this area, it is likely that any time log exercise you underake will confi rm the danger. Again it seems simple, but the correct approach can save a worthwhile amount of time.

47. "IF I HAD WANTED IT TOMORROW I WOULD HAVE ASKED FOR IT TOMORROW"

People can be unreasonable: witness the remark used in the heading here. While many, many things have to be completed by a deadline, it is usually their urgency that causes problems—everything seems to be wanted yesterday (sometimes only because of bad planning) and a cycle of running to keep up ensues.

Deadlines must be addressed realistically. Give yourself sufficient time, build in some contingency, and then you can deal with things properly and still be able to hit a deadline accurately. Fine—or is it? There is another common complication to deadlines: people are dishonest about them. Understandably perhaps—there may be a great deal hanging on hitting one; they affect results and reputations. So what happens is that when something must be done by the end of the month, it is requested for the 25th "to be on the safe side." But this practice, along with the people who do it, becomes known around an office and so the recipient of the deadline assumes that a week later is fine. If several people are involved, then the double-guessing can get worse as misinterpretations are passed on and overall the chances of missing a date increase. It is ironic, but what starts out as a genuine attempt to ensure a deadline is met ends up actually making it less likely that this occurs.

The moral is clear: be honest about deadlines.

In any group with which you are associated, try to make sure the situation about deadlines is clear and open, and that everyone approaches the situation in the same way.

If something needs completing on the 10th of the month, say so. If some contingency is sensible, say so: This has to be completed by the 10th. Let's aim to have it ready two days ahead of this to give time for a last check and make sure there is no chance of our failing to keep our promise to them. Not only does this make it more certain that the deadline involved will be hit, in part because people like the approach and commit to it more wholeheartedly, but it also prevents other things being at risk because time is being spent chasing what is, in fact a fictitious deadline. There is sufficient pressure in most offi ces without compounding the problem artificially.

SELECTED READINGS

Allen, David (2001). *Getting things done: the Art of Stress-Free Productivity*. New York: Viking.

Allen, Kathleen R. (1995). *Time and Information Management that Really Works!* Los Angeles, Calif.: Affinity Publishing

Barling, J., Kelloway, E. K. & Cheung, D. (1996). Time management and achievement striving interact to predict car sale performance. *Journal of Applied Psychology*, 81, 821-826.

Breier, Mark, with Armin A. Brott. (2000). *The 10-Second Internet Maneger: Survive, Thrive and Drive Your Company in the Information Age*. New York, N.Y.: Crown Business.

Claessens, B. J. C., van Erde, W., Rutte, C. G. & Roe, R. A. (2005). A review of the time management literature. *Personnel Review*, 36, 255-276.

Davidson, Jeff. . (2000). *10 Minute Guide to Managing Your Time*. Indianapolis, Ind.: Alpha Books.

Eldeleklioglu, J., Yilmaz, A., & Gultekin, F. (2010). Investigation of teacher trainee's psychological well-being in terms of time management. *Procedia Social and Behavioral Sciences*, 2, 342-348.

Fiore, Neil A (2006). *The Now Habit: A Strategic Program for Overcoming Procrastination and Enjoying Guilt- Free Play*. New York: Penguin Group.

Forster, Mark (2006). *Do It Tomorrow and Other Secrets of Time Management*. Hodder & Stoughton Religious.

Green, L. V., Kolesar, P. J., & Ward, W. (2007). Coping with time-varying demand when setting staffing requirements for a service system. *Production and Operations Management*, 16, 13-39.

Koch, C. J., & Kleinmann, M. (2002). A stitch in time saves nine: Behavioural decision-making explanations for time management problems. *European Journal of Work and Organisational Psychology*, 11(2), 199-217.

Le Blanc, Raymond (2008). *Achieving Objectives Made Easy! Practical goal setting tools & proven time management techniques*. Maarheeze: Cranendonck Coaching.

LeFebvre, K. B. (2009). Prioritize and take stock of you life. *ONS Connect*, 24, 20.

Macan, T. H. (1996). Time management training: Effects on time behaviours, attitudes, and job performance. *Journal of Psychology*, 130, 229-236.

Morgenstern, Julie (2004). *Time Management from the Inside Out: The Foolproof System for Taking Control of Your Schedule—and Your Life* (2nd ed.). New York: Henry Holt/Owl Books.

Mudrack, P. E. (1997). The structure of perceptions of time. *Educational and Psychological Measurement*, 57, 222-240.

Orlikowsky, W. J. & Yates, J. (2002). Its about time: Temporal structuring in organizations. *Organization Science*, 13, 684-700.

Sandberg, Jared (2004). "Though Time-Consuming, To-Do Lists Are a Way of Life". *The Wall Street Journal*.

Saunders, Rebecca M. (2000). "Assertiveness Yourself: How to Say 'No' and Mean It." *Harvard Management Communication Letter*, July, 3(7):9–11. Contains a good assertiveness quiz.

Seo, E. H. (2009). The relationship of procrastination with a mastery goal versus and avoidance goal. *Social Behaviour and Personality*, 37, 911-920.

Walster, Dian. (1993). *Managing Time: A How-To-Do-It Manual for Librarians*. New York, N.Y.: Neal-Schuman.

Weeks, M.J. (1998). *Taking Control with Time Management*, 4th ed. New York, N.Y.: American Management Association. This self-study course is very good.

Other Books on

MANAGEMENT

1. Be a Better Project Manager
2. Be a Better Problem Solver
3. Be a Better Motivator
4. Be a Better Time Manager
5. Effective Director (Guideline)
6. Network Marketing (Guideline)
7. Art of Entrepreneurship
8. How To Beat Your Competitors **(New)**
9. How to Negotiate Effectively **(New)**
10. Art of Advertising **(New)**
11. Art of Marketing **(New)**
12. Art of Growing Business **(New)**
13. Art of Retailing **(New)**
14. Art of Leadership **(New)**
15. Art of Team Building **(New)**
16. Art of Corporate Communication **(New)**
17. Art of Organisational Management **(New)**
18. Improve your Marketing and Grow your Business
19. What Customers Really Want
20. Effective Presentation
21. The Right Decision Every Time
22. Develop Your Decision Making Skills
23. Develop Your Team Building Skills

24. Develop Your Skills to Conduct Effective Meetings
25. How to Export And Import
26. How to Use Money
27. How to Start My Business
28. How to Organise My Office
29. How to Manufacture My Products
30. How to Promote And Advertise
31. How to Sell My Products
32. How to Develop and Maintain Quality

Lotus PRESS

Unit No. 220, 2nd Floor, 4735/22, Prakash Deep Building,
Ansari Road, Darya Ganj, New Delhi- 110002
Ph.: 23280047, 9811838000
E-mail : lotuspress1984@gmail.com, www.lotuspress.co.in